IF I RAN THE COUNTRY

ILLUSTRATED BY **ALLAN SANDERS**

wren
&rook

First published in Great Britain in 2021 by Wren & Rook

ISBN: 978 1 5263 6372 5
E-book ISBN: 978 1 5263 6371 8
10 9 8 7 6 5 4 3

MIX
Paper from
responsible sources
FSC® C104740

Wren & Rook
An imprint of Hachette Children's Group
Part of Hodder & Stoughton
Carmelite House, 50 Victoria Embankment, London EC4Y 0DZ
An Hachette UK Company
www.hachette.co.uk
www.hachettechildrens.co.uk

Printed in the United Kingdom

Managing Editor: Laura Horsley
Senior Editor: Julie Ferris
Art Director: Laura Hambleton
Designed by Nigel Baines

Rich Knight is a BBC journalist. He lives in an upside-down house with his wife, sons, cat and a campervan called Ernie. (Actually, Ernie is parked outside.)

CONTENTS

Hello, **BOSS.** CONGRATULATIONS!

You've just got your hands on a whole new country. (Let's not dwell on how you did that, I don't think I want to know.) How does it feel to be top banana...head honcho...the big cheese...numero uno?

Pretty good, I imagine. But don't get too comfortable. Being in charge is hard work. There are a lot of decisions to be made and not long to make them. If you dawdle, your people might get cross and throw you out – or possibly, if you're really useless, throw you in prison!

(If you're really, really, useless they might storm your presidential palace and chop your head off, but that doesn't happen very often these days.)

BONK

SO, WHAT KIND OF DECISIONS WILL YOU HAVE TO MAKE?

Well ... loads of them. You're in 'politics' now, which means you're in the business of setting up a 'government' to run things.

As leader of a government, you will have the power to make decisions that affect everyone who lives in your country (and sometimes people in other countries too).

You will find yourself making choices about almost everything, from whether to go to war to how old people have to be to get married; from which side of the road cars drive on to how long a school day should be.

Government decisions affect a country's citizens in lots of ways. Governments can make a big difference to how healthy people are, how well educated they are – perhaps even how happy they are.

Let's look on the bright side. It's a big responsibility, yes, but you're not completely on your own. You've got this book. It'll help you figure out what kind of country you want to run (the greatest the world has ever seen, obviously), what kind of leader you want to be and what you believe in.

When leaders make a mess of things, it's usually not because the job is too difficult, but because they've forgotten why they're there. They confuse what's good for them or their friends with what's good for everyone else. We're all trusting you not to make that mistake.

You've left school behind (for now) to become the first child in history to take over the leadership of a modern nation. Very impressive! But taking charge was the easy bit. Now it's time to get down to the difficult business of *being* in charge.

Note to non-leaders: If you've picked up this book by mistake (if you're not already prime minister or president or emperor) keep reading anyway. For one thing: you might be in charge one day. For another: change doesn't always come from the top.

Wherever you are in the world and however unlikely it might seem that you can make a difference, you might be surprised. It's never too early to start arguing for what you believe in. Later, we'll explore how ordinary, puny and powerless citizens like you (not meaning to be rude or anything) can still make change happen.

PART ONE: A BIG QUESTION ?

You might have hoped your first decisions would be choosing which wing of the presidential palace to live in and where to put the hot tub.

But there's a line of advisors queuing up to tell you about important things that need your urgent attention and a teetering tower of papers on your desk which look like origami Jenga®.

Top of the pile is a note from your chief advisor[1] asking a simple question: what sort of government do you want to set up? Have you thought about this yet? Well, now would be a good time to start.

Once you understand more about the different types of government around the world, and how your job might differ depending on which system you choose, you can answer your advisor's question (and then send them off to buy a hot tub).

A good place to start is to ask yourself what kind of government is legitimate and fair.

A government that's 'legitimate' is one that is accepted by the people it governs; in other words, a government that most people think has a right to be in charge (even if they disagree with some of its decisions).

---

1 Most leaders have lots of people around to advise them. Some have a chief or head advisor who stays by their side to help with every decision, like a political best friend. It's probably a good idea, though, to choose experts rather than your actual best friends.

Fair governments listen to their people, take note of their views and try to serve them well.

Think about your head teacher. You might not always like what they say (you might not like them at all) but hopefully you think it's 'legitimate' that they're in charge; they're qualified, experienced and the rest of the teachers seem happy enough with the situation.

If, on the other hand, Keith from Year 7 (the boy who always has egg on his jumper) storms the staffroom and declares himself 'headmaster for life' (despite being 11 years old and having no qualifications whatsoever, not to mention egg on his jumper), you would probably think that he is not a legitimate school leader[2].

Let's whizz through some of the different types of governments you could choose from. Think about which feel fair to you. Then pick one. (And get a move on! That teetering tower of papers on your desk is getting taller by the second.)

---

2 If you suspect your own head teacher is a bit of a Keith, you should probably tell someone.

Democracy

A democracy is a system in which the people who live in a country get to choose who runs it.

They select the government through an election. This is where everyone over a certain age can vote for who they want to be in charge. The elected government works for the people until new leaders are voted in at a future election.

Democracy is formed from two Greek words – *demos*, meaning 'the people', and *kratos*, meaning 'power'[3]. It was invented by the ancient Greeks 2,500 years ago (as you'll see in a moment).

There are a lot of democracies in the world; from Canada to Costa Rica, South Africa to South Korea, the United Kingdom to the United States of America.

---

3 Here's another useful Greek mash-up: 'plutocracy', which comes from *ploutus*, meaning 'rich', and our old friend *kratos*, meaning 'power'. You can probably see where this is going. A plutocracy is a society run by the rich for the benefit of the rich. Does that sound like a fair system?

In fact, roughly half the world's nations are democracies, so there's a pretty good chance you grew up in one.

Democracies are not all the same. There are lots of different versions of the idea. But there are things all democracies have in common.

For example, in democracies people enjoy 'free speech', which means they can say what they think. They can criticise the government as much as they like. Journalists can report all that criticism – without fear of being punished – because democracies enjoy a 'free press'.

If a country is missing either free speech or a free press – or both – it is not a real democracy. (If you're not sure whether the country you grew up in is a democracy, try reading a newspaper or watching the news to see whether people can write and say what they think.)

Real democracies have laws that apply equally to everyone (even the politicians who made them up in the first place). When a democratic government loses an election, it hands its power over to the new winners without sulking.

If you set up your country as a democracy, you'll only be able to stay in charge as long as the people want you there. Sooner or later, they'll vote in someone new and you'll be

out of a job. You might not like the sound of that or the thought of all that criticism.

But perhaps these downsides for you are worth it if you think democracy is the fairest form of government for your citizens? If you decide you are pro-democracy, there are more choices ahead of you. That's because making democracy work is really quite tricky. We'll go into democracy in more detail in a moment. Let's look at some other options first.

Anarchy

Having just got your hands on power, you might not like this idea, because it means letting go of it again. In an anarchy there is no government. Anything goes!

Anarchists say they want organisation from the 'bottom up'; meaning ordinary people (the people at the 'bottom') should be left alone to figure out how to run things without some shouty person at the 'top' (they mean you!) telling everyone what to do.

They think all governments – even ones which start out trying to be fair to everyone – end up taking more power than they really need. Eventually, anarchists say, any government will finish up caring more about rich and powerful people than ordinary citizens.

People who don't like the sound of anarchism worry that without rules and punishments people would start behaving like angry three-year-olds, storming around smashing things and sticking crayons up each other's noses[4].

Anarchists reply that for most of human history there was no government (they're thinking of the time when we were hunter-gatherers, roaming the forests picking berries and spearing rodents), and everything was fine (sort of[5]).

It's hard to picture a modern country with no government. That might be because no one has actually tried it.

Would you like to be the first?

---

4 You probably know this, but sticking crayons up noses is actually really dangerous and definitely not something you should do whether you're an anarchist or not.
5 Well, I mean, I say 'fine', but they *were* eating speared rodents.

Monarchy

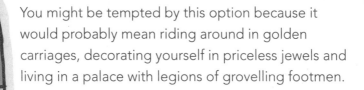

You might be tempted by this option because it would probably mean riding around in golden carriages, decorating yourself in priceless jewels and living in a palace with legions of grovelling footmen.

A king or queen is called a 'monarch' and there are two types: absolute monarchs and constitutional monarchs. In a nutshell: absolute monarchs have **total power** and everyone has to do what they say. A constitutional monarch's power is limited.

Both kinds of monarch are usually born into the job (the monarchy is generally handed down from parent to eldest child) but every royal family tree began somewhere, so you could try to start a new one.

The carriages, jewels and grovelling footmen are usually on offer to both types of monarch so let's look in a little more detail at which might work for you.

Absolute monarchy

An 'absolute monarch' is a king or queen who runs everything. Ordinary people living under an absolute monarch have no say in how they are ruled. There have been all-powerful royals in many places throughout history.

Mansa Musa was a wildly rich king of Mali, West Africa, in the 14th century. He travelled with 12,000 slaves, each carrying a gold bar. He ordered the slaves to give the gold to poor people they met along the way.

There have been powerful Chinese rulers such as Wu Zetian, the only female emperor, who took control in the 7th century by chopping off her rivals' arms and legs and then drowning them in wine.

Are you worried about your rivals, Empress Wu?

Nah – they're 'armless. Glass of wine?[6]

---

6 The publishers apologise for the quality of this joke.

Europe has had lots of serious-looking kings and queens, usually with huge beards. (The queens were less often bearded.) They includes Alfred the Great of England, the Great Knut of Denmark and Catherine the Great of Russia. Eventually, however, people being ruled by monarchs in Europe began to wonder whether their kings and queens were really so great. About 150 years ago, they kicked a bunch of absolute monarchs off their thrones and sometimes killed them too (just to be sure they got the message).

There are only a handful of absolute monarchies still around (in Oman and Saudi Arabia in the Middle East, for example). Could you make it work? Possibly. Is it a fair and legitimate form of government? Well, that's for you to decide.

Constitutional monarchy

A constitutional monarch is a king or queen who – despite looking like they're in charge – has to stick to the rules of a constitution[7] which limits what they can do.

The king or queen is 'head of state'[8] in a constitutional monarchy, but they are not head of the government. That means a constitutional monarchy can also be a democracy. Sweden, Thailand, the United Kingdom, the Netherlands, Japan and Denmark are all examples of constitutional monarchies which are also democracies.

Constitutional monarchs do have some power. If the prime minister goes bananas and even their own friends in parliament want to get rid of them, the king or queen may be able to step in and ask someone else to take over. (A parliament is a place where individuals elected by the people meet to discuss and vote on laws.)

Most of the time, however, constitutional monarchs try their very best to stay out of politics. That gives them more time for the kinds of hobbies constitutional monarchs enjoy (such as horse riding and darts).

---

7 A 'constitution' is a set of instructions (often written down) which explain a country's rules. Some constitutions evolve over time. Some are worked out all at once. You're going to need one for your own country. I suggest getting a team together to work on this as soon as possible!
8 The main representative of a nation, but not necessarily its real boss.

Dictatorship

Dictators are individuals with total control over their country (like an absolute monarch, except they aren't royalty and were not born into the job). People living under a dictator, like those living under an absolute monarch, have no say in how they are ruled.

Sometimes dictators take power by force (a 'coup'). Sometimes they win an election more or less fairly and then – surprise! – reveal themselves to be a dictator.

People living under a dictatorship are in for a difficult time. Dictators ignore the rights[9] of individuals and try to control everyone's lives. They don't allow criticism, and they attack anyone who opposes them.

They use TV, newspapers and social media to spread 'propaganda' (lies presented as real information) to make themselves look good.

Dictators have started wars with neighbours and imprisoned or even killed many of their own people.

---

9 Rights are basic freedoms which people think everyone should have automatically – the right to life, say, or the right not to be sent to prison for something you didn't do.

Occasionally a dictator comes along who says they are a 'benevolent dictator'. "Okay," they're saying, "yes, I'm a dictator, but I'm a nice one who's only trying to help." So far, that's never been true.

There have been some really terrible dictators. Adolf Hitler, who led Germany into the Second World War, was one of the worst.

Hitler started a war in which about 85 million people died. He also hated Jewish people. During a period called the Holocaust, he killed six million Jews – men, women and children – before Germany lost the war and he was stopped.

Dictators are sometimes called 'autocrats' or 'authoritarians' and there are still some in power today, for example in North Korea. Whatever you call them, do you think they pass the fairness test?

SO HOW DOES DEMOCRACY WORK?

If after reading the last few pages you've chosen democracy as your leadership style, you're not alone. Lots of other leaders have made the same choice. But the decisions don't stop there. In a democracy people express their opinion by voting. **The first question you need to ask yourself is this: should you give everyone a say on everything?** That's called 'direct democracy'.

Every time you need to make a decision in a direct democracy you ask all the people what they think using a process called a 'referendum'. You then go along with what the majority (more than half) say they want.

This is how the ancient Greeks did it when they invented democracy[10]. These days, though, the only country in the world that tries to run things a bit like this is Switzerland.

Swiss people have lots of opportunities to say what they think through referendums. They also have lots of opportunities to go skiing and eat melted cheese, but that's not strictly relevant.

A direct democracy is an attempt to be very fair. But there are some downsides.

What if the thing people are being asked to decide is really complicated and most voters haven't taken the time to understand it? What if hardly anyone votes and so the result doesn't represent the views of a majority of citizens but only a majority of the people who bothered to vote? And if the majority always get their way, does that mean the minority (the smaller group) never do? And, if so, is *that* fair?

10 Democracy was developed in Athens in ancient Greece, but their system was very different to the systems used now. The Athenians would choose 500 random people and put them in charge for a year! When these people came up with a (random) new law, everyone else could vote on it at a public assembly. People were encouraged to take part by officials flicking paint-covered ropes at them.

Imagine the majority of Swiss people think schools should serve melted cheese (and nothing else!) every lunchtime. Now let's say a minority of Swiss schoolchildren get ill if they eat cheese.

Is it fair that the majority should get what it wants – in this case melted cheese – even though what's good for them is bad for a minority? (For the record: the Swiss government does not force unwilling children to eat cheese, melted or otherwise.)

The alternative to direct democracy and the melted cheese problem is 'representative democracy'. In a representative democracy people don't vote on every question. They vote for someone to answer those questions for them.

One way to do this is to divide up the country into smaller areas called 'constituencies' or 'districts', and ask the people living in each of those constituencies to choose one person to represent them. These representatives go to a parliament to make laws and generally run the country.

The representatives are left to get on with it for a few years before facing the voters again. If the voters don't like what their representative did in parliament, they can choose to send someone else next time.

This system allows everyone else to get on with their lives and pay less attention to politics. Meanwhile, the representatives are supposed to think about the interests of everyone in their constituency and not just those who voted for them.

(They might, for example, look at the clash between melted-cheese eaters and melted-cheese haters and conclude that schools should serve vegan hot dogs instead.)

No system is perfect, however, and a representative democracy has downsides too. The most obvious one is that, between elections, ordinary people have very little say about things. They just have to hope their representative is doing a good job. If you have decided to set up your country as a democracy you are going to have to decide whether you think direct or representative democracy is the best system. Here's another question:

How do you create a system which gives a leader or a government enough power to do its job, but not so much power that the people in charge can do whatever comes into their heads – however stupid – without any way to stop them?

 # The answer is checks and balances.

The phrase is often used to describe the system of government in the United States, but any proper democracy has some form of this idea built into it.

The idea of checks and balances is to create different sources of political power, which are separate from each other and which have some control over each other.

In the US there are three branches of government: **executive** (the president); **legislative** (representatives from each district); and **judicial** (judges).

The legislative branch can make laws but the president can block them.
The president can issue orders but the legislative branch can block them.
The judicial branch can look at all these laws and orders and declare them illegal (which blocks them).

Imagine the law-makers in the legislative branch decide to ban cats from the country (under pressure from bird-lovers).

The president cancels that law (he loves cats) but gives an order banning dogs (which he's hated ever since the President of France let her poodle poo on his lawn when she came to visit).

The judges in the Supreme Court would rush back from playing crazy golf and eating burgers (or whatever judges do for fun) and consult the constitution (the rules of the country) to help them make a decision. Now, imagine that the constitution states, **'The People shall have the right to keep cats for the purposes of furry companionship'.**

The judges would rule that the cat ban was illegal (because it conflicted with the constitution) but the dog ban was fine.

What's useful about 'checks and balances' like this is that if the president turns out to be a power-crazed maniac, or the law-makers in the legislature turn out to be a whole bunch of power-crazed maniacs, wiser heads elsewhere can do something about it.

How to pick people for parliament:

If you're planning to set up your country as a 'representative democracy' then you will have to choose a voting system for deciding who gets sent to parliament.

There are professors who do nothing but study voting systems trying to figure out which is the best. It can get very complicated.

Let's look at two popular choices. The **'first past the post'** system and **'proportional representation'**.

Imagine you create a parliament with 300 'seats' (which just means the parliament has 300 members). Each seat represents one part of the country (a constituency). Voters get to choose at election time who should represent that constituency in parliament.

Let's say there are three main parties in your system: the Pinks, the Purples and the Yellows.

There are two kinds of political parties. There are parties, with cake and crisps and dancing, where people who like politics hang out together. Then there are organisations called political parties made up of people who share a similar political point of view. If you're going to set yourself up as a democracy, you're probably going to need some of the second type.

You might have heard of the Republicans in the United States, the Liberal Party in Australia or the Labour Party in the United Kingdom. There are many more. Parties are a good way to organise a large number of people around a set of political ideas.

In a 'parliamentary democracy', parties organise candidates at election time and try to get as many of their own people as possible voted in to parliament.

In a **'first past the post' (FPTP)** system, a party needs a majority of those 300 seats to win. So if the Purples get 151 or more seats, they have won. They get to form the government. If no party gets a majority, however, things are trickier. A group of parties might be able to join forces to create a majority (say if the Pinks and Yellows have 151 seats or more between them and agree to work together). This is called a 'coalition'.

FPTP is the system used in the UK, the US, Canada, India and several African nations.

One problem with this system is that many voters don't get what they want. Think about it this way: if the Purples have 151 seats, that's 149 seats where Pinks or Yellows won. That's a LOT of people who voted Pink and Yellow, who aren't going to be very happy with the results.

The Pink and Yellow representatives will be in parliament. They will be able to challenge the Purple government there. But they won't be part of the government.

In fact, it's worse than that. Imagine an election in a constituency where the Purple candidate wins with 10,000 votes but the Pink candidate only just loses with 9,999 votes.

The Purple candidate goes to parliament and the Pink candidate goes home. That's a whopping 9,999 voters who didn't get what they want.

'Proportional representation' (PR) is designed to deal with this problem. In a PR system, instead of voting for a candidate in your constituency, you just vote for a party. If the Pinks win a third of all votes across the country, they then get a third of all seats in parliament. This means everyone's vote counts. Most European countries use some form of proportional representation.

The PR system makes it very hard for one party to win on its own. That means a coalition is likely to be needed to form a government.

Some think coalitions are a good thing, not only because every vote counts, but also because they bring lots of different views and perspectives into government and rely on politicians looking for ways to compromise and agree.

People who don't like the PR system, however, say that since coalitions are made up of several different parties who might not like each other much, it's hard for them to get things done.

Politicians in a coalition government, they say, will spend too much time arguing with each other and storming out of meeting rooms.

There may be no perfect option. But as a democratic leader (if that's what you have decided you are) you will have to pick one anyway.

Should children be allowed to vote?

No country in the world allows children under 16 to vote.
A handful of countries – Argentina, Austria, Brazil, Ecuador,
Malta, Nicaragua, Scotland and Wales – allow people to start
voting at 16. In almost every other democracy you have to be
18 to vote. And in a few countries, such as Cameroon, you
have to be even older. Why? Some argue that children don't
know enough about the world to make sensible decisions.

**Hang on old timer, adults
have made some pretty
terrible decisions. Would
we really do any worse?**

If you think children should be
allowed to vote, you're not alone.
One politics professor recently
argued that the voting age should
be lowered to six. The more
voters there are, he said, the better democracy works.

There was a time when women or people who didn't own
property were not allowed to vote. Things only changed
when those people pointed out how unfair that was and
started demanding the vote. You might have heard of the
Suffragettes, for example, who argued that women should
be allowed to vote in Britain. They succeeded in 1918.

33

Giving the vote to more people can make government fairer because if a government wants to win an election, it needs to appeal to as many voters as possible. After 1918, for example, governments could no longer ignore the views of women without losing votes.

So perhaps it does make sense to include the one big group of citizens who still have no say in how they're governed in any democratic country: children.

Children might be given the attention they deserve by governments if they can tell their leaders what they think by voting. But would a six year old vote for serious things like fixing the environment? Or mad things like introducing alligators to park ponds?

As leader of a brand new nation you'll have to decide who gets the vote and at what age. You might think giving children the vote is a risk (because of the alligator thing) but you might think the real risk is letting adults continue to keep the vote to themselves.

SO, BIG SHOT, WHAT'S IT GOING TO BE?

Perhaps you don't really like any of these systems. Most leaders take charge of a government that's been around for centuries. You're lucky enough to be starting from scratch. That gives you a chance to try something new.

You could make big decisions by tossing a coin (at least that way you'd be right half the time) or mash up other Greek words to see what you get. How about a hippocracy[11]? That's government by and for the benefit of horses.

I think it's fair to say, however, that most people think plain old democracies are likely to work better than government by horse and likely to be fairer than, say, a dictatorship.

But while there isn't (as far as I know) a country anywhere in the world with a horse in charge[12], there are unfair governments in the world and there always have been. Why?

---

11 Hippocracy comes from the Greek *hippos*, meaning 'horse', and, yes, *kratos*, meaning 'power'. You should probably forget you ever heard it, because I just made it up. (And it's silly.)

12 The Roman Emperor Caligula is said to have tried to make his favourite horse a 'consul', which was one of the most important roles in the empire. That might be the closest any horse has come to government.

Well, you know why don't you? Don't pretend you haven't thought about it! You're in charge now (the top dog!) and wouldn't it be fun to do whatever you like?

You could make everyone call you Most Excellent Empress of Everything and build yourself a massive fort with canons that shoot balls of buffalo bogey at anyone who disagrees with you.

You could have any adult who dares call an end to screen time taken down to your dank dungeons and flogged by warty henchmen with hairs sticking out of their nostrils.

It's possible that you decided many pages ago that democracy is for wimps, fairness is for losers and that you plan to be a ruthless dictator with a to-do list that includes imprisoning everyone who laughed at you that time when you split your shorts in PE.

But if you want what's best for everyone, and not just for you, you'll need to think about what your people want and need. **Here's an idea. Why not start a list of what you think those things might be?**

Is it freedom? Happiness? Safety? Do they want to be able to get rich? Do they want someone else to get on with running the country, so they don't have to worry about it, or do they want to have their say?

Now think again about each system we've talked about (and any other system you might have invented), and ask yourself which fits best with what you think is important to your citizens.

Don't lose that piece of paper. Later on we'll try to figure out what you believe in – the values you stand for – and this list will be a good place to start.

NEW COUNTRY 'TO DO' LIST

As well as making big decisions, you need to find some time to get creative. Countries need things such as flags, bank notes and national anthems. Someone's going to have to design and compose all this stuff for your country. Who better to do that than you? You'll find one of these tasks at the end of every chapter.
The first item on your 'to-do' list is an obvious one:
give your country a name.

What's in a name?

A country's name usually stretches back into distant history, so creating one from scratch is quite difficult. But there are recent examples of countries choosing new names. Namibia in southwest Africa was called – er – 'South West Africa' until it got a shiny new name. Why 'Namibia'? Because a large part of this very beautiful country is covered by the Namib Desert.

Perhaps you should sketch a map of your country, including all its most important features (rivers, mountains, deserts, volcanoes, roller coasters … whatever you've got), and see if you can create your country's name from any of those?

Or you could just name the country after yourself. This is a slightly big-headed thing to do, but you would not be the first to do it. Quite a few countries are named after individuals, including Bolivia (Simón Bolívar), Saudi Arabia (Muhammad bin Saud), Colombia (Christopher Columbus) and the United States of America (Amerigo Vespucci). In 2018 Swaziland's ruler, King Mswati III, renamed the country after himself, calling it eSwatini. He did so, he said, because he was tired of people confusing Swaziland with Switzerland (even though they are about 7,000 miles apart and people in eSwatini don't eat much melted cheese).

TOP SECRET: MEMO FROM THE DESK OF THE LEADER

Grab yourself a piece of paper and start noting down the decisions you've made so far. You could write it out as follows …

With the power vested in me as leader, I have decided to call our new nation:

[It's really tempting to name the country after yourself, isn't it? I won't lie. If I was in charge, I would definitely be calling it Richlandia.]

and to set it up as a:

Democracy/Anarchy/Dictatorship[13]/ Absolute monarchy/Constitutional monarchy

The next section only applies if you have chosen to set up a democracy.

My democracy will be:

Direct/Representative

---

13 Seriously? Are you *sure*?

The Voting System will be:

First past the post/proportional representation

I will give the vote to anyone over

[Here's where you decide how low you will go: 18 years old, like most countries, or younger.]

years of age

If you've decided to create an entirely new system of government, you might need a bigger piece of paper!

PART TWO: WHO WILL YOU WORK WITH?

This section is about your team and your relationships with other countries. You can't run your country on your own, there's too much to do. And your country can't fix global problems on its own, they're too big.

You're going to have to work out who you can trust and who will bring the skills and experience you need to your team.

You'll be spending a lot of time with your team so I would avoid choosing anyone with irritating habits.

You will also need to work out which countries will be your allies (friends) and you should keep your eyes open for potential enemies[14] too.

Your team

Most governments divide up the task of running the country into separate departments. You'd still be in charge if you choose to do this, but each department would be led by someone who reports to you.

---

14 There are lots of reasons why two countries might be enemies. They could be arguing about who really owns some land (Pakistan and India both think a region called Kashmir is part of their country, for example). There may be other historical reasons why two countries distrust or dislike each other (like the US and Iran) but they are too complicated for a humble footnote.

These department bosses are usually called ministers or secretaries. Together they form your top team. You can call them your cabinet or your central committee – or anything you like, really.

You're going to have to decide which departments you want. Here are a few you might think about including:

Treasury department

The important people in this department are responsible for looking after your country's economy. (In other words: how money is made and how it is spent.) The treasury will decide how much money to collect from your citizens in taxes[15] and how to share out that money among other government

---

15 We'll come back to tax later. It's quite important. It is money a government collects from its citizens to pay for everything from buying warships to putting up streetlights.

departments who will then spend it on the things you, the leader, want (like schools, hospitals and chocolate fountains). Governments borrow money from banks or other countries when taxes alone can't cover everything. Most leaders make the head of their treasury responsible for borrowing money and making sure the country can afford to pay it back. Your Treasury Secretary[16] might also be in charge of keeping the economy growing (in other words: making sure the country is getting richer rather than poorer) by helping businesses succeed.

[16] You can call the boss of your treasury anything you like, because it's your country. If you want to play it safe, however, 'Treasury Secretary' will probably do. That's the title used in the US. The UK calls the boss of its treasury 'The Chancellor of the Exchequer'. 'Finance Minister' is another option.

Foreign office or state department

The job of this department is to build relationships with other countries and to look after people from your country when they go abroad. The team in this department will oversee a network of offices in other capital cities called 'embassies'. Your embassy staff will be able to help you understand other countries, trade

with them and form alliances[17]. If citizens of your country get into trouble somewhere else (if they are robbed, say, or they fall ill), they can go to their embassy for help. And if you have a team of spies[18] to snoop on other countries, it would probably make sense to ask the boss of your foreign department to run it.

---

17 Alliances are a bit like friendships between nations. We'll get into all that in more detail on page 72.
18 Leaders don't like to admit how much spying goes on, but the truth is just about every country does it. Your spies might help keep your country safe (if, for example, they find out that some other country or group is planning to attack it) or they might just help you make friends with the leader next door by finding out what they want for Christmas. "Oh, that was so thoughtful! Would you like to form an alliance?"

Home office or interior ministry

The serious people in this department run the police, courts and prisons.

That means they have the power to catch you and lock you up if you break the law. They also control the borders. Borders are the edges of your country. If your country is an island, it's pretty simple. The border is the sea. If you share a land border with another country, however, you might need to put up a sign. (Some leaders think it would be even better to build a wall, but hopefully  that won't be necessary.) Either way, you will need staff to keep an eye on who's coming in and who's going out. And if you want to limit who comes in[19], it will be this bunch who're doing the limiting.

---

19 People moving to another country are called 'immigrants'. Some people are pleased to see immigrants coming to their country – especially when they are doing so to escape danger elsewhere – but others worry that too much immigration will be bad news. This is a particularly sensitive issue so we'll talk more about it on page 99.

Defence department

These guys might be even more serious than the people who work in your interior ministry. This is where the heads of your armed forces work, along with people from your government whose job it is to manage the military. Most countries have an air force, an army, a navy and perhaps a few other things like marines and special forces. These are hugely complicated organisations with a lot of expensive equipment (have you seen the price of a jet fighter?) and it takes a lot of work to run them. If you're a peaceful sort of person you might well be wondering whether you really need the ability to wage war on a huge scale. Well, the thing is, you might not be planning to attack anyone. But it's always possible someone else is planning to attack you. (That's why it's called a defence department[20].)

---

20 Call it a War Office if you want to make your neighbours nervous.

Education department

You can probably guess what goes on here. Looking after schools, colleges and universities is a big job and an important one. You're no longer in school, of course, because you're busy pursuing your frankly incredible career as a national leader. But think of the classmates you left behind. They deserve good schools, well-trained teachers and an opportunity to get ahead in life through learning. Those things can't happen without a big team of clever and committed people working hard to create an education system that helps everyone. Staff here will be responsible for making sure teaching staff are well-qualified (we don't want any Keiths, do we?), figuring out

what children and students should learn, and making sure schools, colleges and universities have the money they need to teach properly in safe and comfortable buildings. Come to think of it, this department might be the most important one of all. I'd think about putting some of your best people here.

Environment department

Later in this book (page 137) we're going to think about climate change, which is a global problem you should probably get working on alongside other world leaders. Climate change has become so serious that all countries are going to have to make big changes if they are to be part of the solution. We'll talk about what those changes might be later on. But, for now, make a note that if you are serious about tackling climate change then you're going to have to give some of your best and brightest people a

department to work on it. But that may not be all they do. You might want to look after or clean up your own country by lowering pollution, restoring forests, purifying rivers, clearing litter and cutting down the use of plastic. All those important tasks would also be the responsibility of your environment department. So, again, this is a big job.

You might well need other departments. How about a health department, for example, to look after your hospitals, a transport department to run the trains, and a farming department to, well, help your farmers (and to make sure they're feeding everyone properly).

Your departments will reflect what you think is important. You can have as many as you need. So don't be afraid to create some completely new ones.

Perhaps you plan to replace roads and trains with a huge network of log flumes. If so, you're going to need a Log Flume Department. (If you do this, by the way, I want you to tell everyone it was my idea.)

When you've decided which departments you need, you should start thinking about who to put in charge of them.

I'd like to introduce you to a man called Abraham Lincoln who was President of the United States of America from 1861 to 1865. Lincoln was a great leader, despite having no interest (as far as we know) in log flumes.

When he won the presidency it was a surprise to a lot of people. There were more famous candidates who expected to beat him.

They did not like losing to this strange-looking man in a silly hat[21] with far less experience.

---

21 Lincoln wore a tall black 'stovepipe' hat which did look a little silly – partly because he was a very tall man even without his hat – but it had the advantage of making him instantly recognisable.

Lincoln needed to appoint a cabinet. He knew that the best men available to join his team were the unhappy bunch he had just beaten to the top job. (They were all men because women weren't even allowed to vote back then).

He must have been tempted to ignore them and to choose less qualified people who would be more likely to do what he said without argument.

But Lincoln resisted that temptation and offered top jobs to his fiercest rivals. Why? Because he wanted clever people around him who would hold a range of different opinions and who would not be afraid to argue with him.

Lincoln knew that he would not always be right. He wanted people to look for problems with his arguments. He knew that a team prepared to challenge him would make better decisions than a team that always agreed with him.

Abe Lincoln quickly earned the respect and loyalty of his talented team-mates because he listened carefully to what they had to say, shared credit when things went well and accepted a share of the blame when things went badly. **Perhaps we should all be a little more like Abe!**

Lincoln would tell you to surround yourself with the best and cleverest people you know and listen to them - even if you have an uncomfortable feeling that some might be better and cleverer than you!

A cabinet like that won't always agree with each other, or with you. In the end, of course, it will be your job to make the final decision. Sometimes that will feel lonely. But your decisions will probably be better and stronger if you've considered the opinions of others first.

Your decision-making will get even better still if you make an effort to appoint a team of people who are not only prepared to argue with you, but who are different from you.

People with different life experiences will be able to help you see or understand things you might otherwise miss. Your government is likely to do a better job for everyone in your country if it is representative of all the different kinds of people who live there. That means pulling together a team which reflects the different backgrounds of the wider population.

You can't possibly understand everything or know how the world looks from every perspective on your own. If you appoint the right team, you won't have to.

Here's a good story which proves why expanding your team to include people who don't think like you can be very helpful. (Well, I think it's a good story. You might think differently.)

During the Second World War, the US Air Force was losing a lot of bomber planes. They were being shot down by enemy fighters. The solution? Add armour to the planes. But adding armour everywhere would make the planes too heavy to fly. So where should they put it?

The solution was simple. Look at the planes when they came back from missions, see where they're most damaged by bullet holes, and add armour to those sections. Clever, right?

But the Air Force officers, despite all agreeing with each other, also agreed that they should invite other people – with different experience and knowledge – to look at the problem too. So they invited a bunch of mathematicians to join them.

One of the mathematicians was a man called Abraham Wald who took one look at the bullet-riddled planes said: "You have it exactly the wrong way round![22]".

The planes they were looking at had made it back to base despite being damaged in some places, he explained. That meant planes could be hit in those places and still fly.

There were no planes with bullet holes in other places because planes hit there hadn't made it home. Therefore, Wald said, the armour should go not where there were bullet holes but where there were no bullet holes. He was right, wasn't he?

By including someone with a different way of thinking in their decision-making, the US Air Force made a better decision.

As leader, it may not be enough to pull together a team of people with different backgrounds, experience and ideas. You also need to make sure everyone in that team has a chance to say what they think. You may have noticed (perhaps even in your old life as a school pupil) that some people are much happier speaking up than others.

---

22 History does not record what he really said. He might have said: "OMG! Seriously?".

But it's very often the case that quieter people – those less likely to put their hands up – have at least as much to contribute as their noisier colleagues.

So when you're in charge of a team or a meeting – whether it's your cabinet or just your classmates – try to be careful to make sure everyone gets an opportunity to express their opinion, even those who need your encouragement to do so.

Working with other countries

Although the world is quite a big place, it feels smaller and smaller all the time. A perilous journey by ship which once took weeks or even months – interrupted by mutinies, scurvy, plank-walking and sharks – can now be made in hours by plane (preferably not one riddled with bullet holes).

These days we don't even really need to bother with the plane (which isn't much more comfortable than sailing with a mutinous, scurvy-riddled crew anyway). We can appear on screen on the other side of the world in seconds.

The world is inter-connected and it simply isn't possible for any one country to cut itself off from the others. Even North Korea, which has tried to cut itself off from the rest of the world, and is sometimes called the 'hermit kingdom', relies on trade with China to survive.

This section will help you figure out how to deal with other countries – trading with them, forming military alliances with them and co-operating with them.

Trade or raid

Anyone who's ever collected football stickers or Pokémon® cards knows the basics of trade. You want a card someone else has, they want one you have, so you trade.

Trade between nations, or between merchants from different parts of the world, isn't so different. And it has been going on for a long time – since well before anyone had thought of Pokémon® cards.

China traded with Rome 2,000 years ago, carrying luxuries along the 'Silk Road'.

Centuries ago, European explorers scoured the world looking for new lands – new to them, at least[23] – and brought home crazy-looking things that Europeans had never seen before (like tomatoes) and began trading them across the high seas.

Most people think that trade is a good thing. One argument in favour of it is that in the end it helps to create peace.

Think back to that highly desirable Pokémon® card.

As well as trade, there are other less peaceful ways you could get hold of the card you desire. You could simply steal it when no-one is looking (or, if you're an unusually horrible and brutish person, attack the card's owner and take it by force).

That kind of thing – on a country-to-country level – has certainly happened many times in history (as we'll see on the next page).

---

23 Wherever these Europeans went in search of 'new' lands they found people who already lived there. There was nothing new about those places to their original inhabitants. But the Europeans, who had better weapons, often ignored or attacked the locals and claimed ownership of their territories.

Trading peacefully is a better strategy in the long term. You can only take a Pokémon® card by force once or twice. Pretty soon, no-one will let you anywhere near their cards again.

If you trade fairly, however, people will trust you and you'll be able to keep swapping cards for a long time.

Few (possibly no) countries trade Pokémon® cards. But the idea is exactly the same. I need silk, which you have. You need spices, which I have. Let's swap! You need oil, which I have, I need cotton, which you have. Swapsies? I need the Charmeleon card, you need Pikachu, do we have a deal?

(Okay, this is a terrible example. No-one would really give up Charmeleon for Pikachu.)

 # The darker side of trade

Trade has helped to create peace between countries. But there have been times when the desire of one group to get its hands on stuff belonging to another has had darker consequences.

From the 15th century onwards, Europeans went in search of lands to conquer or colonise[24]. They created empires of these lands and helped themselves to the riches they found there.

The British created the most powerful of these empires. As recently as 100 years ago, the British Empire controlled about a quarter of the world, including India and a big chunk of Africa.

It started to unravel quickly after the Second World War – which had left Britain weak after years of fighting – when first India and then many other countries broke away from the empire to become independent nations.

Some say the British Empire helped make the countries it controlled more modern – for example by building railways or schools – but most people these days agree that it was wrong for one country to dominate so many others, taking resources and treating the people who lived there as inferior.

There was one kind of trade that several European empire-building nations relied on that was particularly horrible: slavery.

Britain, Portugal, Spain, France, Holland and Denmark took people from Africa by force and shipped them

---

24 When one bunch of people invade and take control of land that does not belong to them, they have 'conquered' it. When they send people to settle and live in that territory, as well as taking political control, they have 'colonised' it.

to the Americas where they were made to work tirelessly without pay.

Many Europeans became very rich trading slaves and the practice carried on into the 19th century. (The United States abolished slavery in 1865 thanks, in part, to our old friend Abraham Lincoln.)

Country clubs

You might want to think about applying for membership of a club of nations.

There are quite a few of them: **the Shanghai Cooperation Organisation, the Arab League, the African Union, the Nordic Council, the Council of the Baltic Sea States** and several more.

Most of these groups were set up so that leaders from nearby countries could meet to talk about problems they have in common and enjoy driving around each other's capital cities in limousines.

There's one club of nations which has become much more than that: **the European Union.** It also proves the point that trade between nations can help to create peace.

After the Second World War (when neighbouring European countries fought each other), Europe's leaders were determined to prevent a third, so they came up with a clever idea.

In 1952 they formed an organisation called the **European Coal and Steel Community**, which included the former enemies France and Germany.

This new organisation agreed to share their coal and steel. The countries in the community would have to co-operate to get their hands on both.

This was a very good idea because you couldn't fight a war without steel (which was needed to make tanks and ships) or coal (which powered the factories that built them).

Now France and Germany would have to co-operate to prepare for a war. And they were hardly likely to do that if the war they were preparing for was against each other. It totally worked. There hasn't been another war between these nations.

The European Coal and Steel Community has since grown and changed a lot. Today it's evolved into the European Union (EU), which is a club of 27 nations.

The EU 27 trade freely together[25] and give each other's citizens the right to travel and live anywhere in the club. They work together to help poorer EU regions catch up with richer ones.

---

25 This means the 27 EU nations can buy (import) and sell (export) things to each other without any tariffs (tax added by governments to imports and exports), quotas (limits imposed by governments on how much stuff can be imported and exported) or other barriers (rules which might make it harder to sell things made in one country to customers in another). This makes it much easier and cheaper for businesses within the EU to operate in all EU countries and has made lots of EU businesses – and EU countries – richer than they would otherwise have been.

There were once 28 EU members but at the end of 2019, the UK left.

There had been a referendum (remember those?) and a majority of voters said they wanted to leave. People voted to leave for lots of different reasons, but many thought the EU had become too big and too bossy.

But what's all this got to do with you and your country?

Well, you'll have to decide: **how closely do you want to work with your neighbours? Do you want to be in a club benefiting from working together, even though the club might sometimes make decisions you don't agree with? Or would you prefer to go it alone?**

It's a bit like being in a gang. Not a scary criminal gang - hopefully you're not a member of one those - but a gang of friends. You feel stronger together. But sometimes you have to go along with the gang's plans even though you'd prefer to do something else. Is it worth it?

The dream of world government

If an alien force arrived just beyond our atmosphere, threatening to take over the world, we would probably forget about the differences (if there are any) between the people of Austria and the people of Australia, or the people of Mali and the people of Malta, and freak out equally everywhere as one species: humans.

The idea that we are one people has led some towards the idea of a 'world government'.

This hasn't happened yet, but the world has taken some small steps towards it.

After the **First World War (1914–1918)**, the victorious countries led the creation of a new organisation called **The League of Nations.**

The idea was that member countries would work together to stop international arguments getting out of hand and so avoid another horrific war.

It went pretty well at first. When the Swedes and the Finns started squaring up for a fight in 1921 over some islands both claimed as their own, for example, the League of Nations stepped in and helped them reach an agreement.

But as you know, the First World War is called the First World War for a reason… there was a second one.

The world started hurtling towards war again in the 1930s and the League of Nations was powerless to stop it. The experiment had failed, and the League of Nations closed.

You're more likely to have heard of the United Nations (UN) which came next because the UN is still around. It was formed in 1945 after the Second World War ended.

The UN is based in New York City and pretty much every country in the world is a member. Like the League of Nations, the UN's main role is to promote international peace and to help sort out arguments between members.

Lots of wars have happened since 1945 – sadly there are some happening right now – so the UN hasn't completely worked. But it has had successes. It has kept peace in many parts of the world, delivered food aid to people who need it and helped countries to work together.

You will have to decide whether to apply for membership of the United Nations. At the very least, it might give you a good excuse to travel from your new country to the US from time to time. (Who doesn't love hanging out in New York?)

Military alliances

Countries that are allies are friends; they either share a similar view of the world, or they recognise that they could help each other out.

It's not all that different from real friendship. (You and your best friend know that if you stick together when the school bully tries to raid your lunch boxes, you'll both have more chance of holding on to your crisps that day.)

You might have heard of **NATO (the North Atlantic Treaty Organisation),** a huge military alliance which was created in 1949 during the Cold War[26].

The rules of NATO membership are simple and summed up in Article 5 of its founding treaty which says (more or less): pick on any one of us, and we will all fight back together.

---

26 The Cold War lasted from 1947 to around 1990. It was a period when a group of western capitalist nations (all members of NATO and led by the US) stood together against a group of communist nations (led by the Soviet Union, which was mainly Russia, and members of a military alliance called the Warsaw Pact). We'll talk about the differences between capitalism and communism later. These two powerful military alliances did not actually go to war against each other directly (there were smaller wars fought through their friends) but they came close to it several times.

If you like the sound of NATO, there's a helpful video on its website called 'How does a country join NATO'.

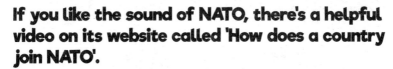

You don't have to join the NATO alliance, of course. You could form your own international friendships. Have a look at a map of the world, find your country on it, and think about who you could pick.

Maybe you want to make friends with the country next door? Perhaps you want to cosy up to the biggest and most powerful country in case some other nation starts pushing you around one day.

You could even make friends with countries you'd quite like to visit – sunny places, perhaps, with good beaches – since you are bound to have to visit your allies from time to time. Or you might find yourself drawn to countries that speak the same language as you.

If it all sounds a bit like how it works in the playground (sticking together with a few friends for safety and support) that's because it is. And – just like in the playground – alliances go both ways.

You might form an alliance with a country you hope will stick by you when you need help. In return, you will need to be ready to stick by your allies when *they* need help. That's the deal with alliances (and, of course, friendships).

NEW COUNTRY 'TO DO' LIST:

Design a flag

Every country has a flag. They're a kind of national logo. They come in all colours and patterns and many feature dragons, stars, lions or birds. They were invented thousands of years ago as military banners when armies carried them into battle.

You have a great opportunity to design a flag which looks completely unlike everyone else's. After all, you want your country's flag to be eye-catching, don't you? Why not have a go now? (Pro tip: felt tip pens will make a mess in this book. It's the wrong kind of paper. I suggest you design your flag on a separate sheet.)

All flags rely on symbolism – colours or images which mean something – so you could think about what you want your flag to say about your country. (Although you could just choose a design that looks cool!)

A rising sun, for example, might symbolise a hopeful future. White might symbolise peace. A poo emoji, on the other hand, would look hilarious – but what would it say about your country?

Some countries choose to show their national animal on their flag. If you haven't picked one of those yet, it's time to get thinking. (Might I recommend a pangolin[27], by the way? No country in the world has adopted the pangolin as its national animal.)

---

27 Pangolins are scaly mammals that look a bit like anteaters. They live in Africa and Asia. Pangolins are hunted and threatened with extinction. Pangolins received some good news in 2016, however, when almost every country in the world agreed to try to save them. This is a pretty good example of what can be achieved when countries choose to work together.

TOP SECRET: MEMO FROM THE DESK OF THE LEADER

Grab another piece of paper and note down the decisions you made in this section. You could copy the template on the next page.

With the power vested in me as leader I have decided our new flag will look like this:

[When you've sketched your flag, it would be a good idea to explain what it symbolises (what the colours and shapes you have chosen represent). You could find inspiration by looking online at other countries' flags (Bhutan's is my favourite).]

and our government will include the following departments:

[This is where you list the teams you need to do the things you think are important – like the treasury, education and log flume departments.]

I intend to appoint the following people to my team:

[Who would you like alongside you as you lead your nation forwards? You could describe the kinds of people you need (the qualities or experience you are looking for) or actual people you know.]

I intend to create alliances with the following countries:

[It might help to know where your country is on the world map. Perhaps start by looking at an atlas and figuring that out.]

Our nation will seek membership of:

The United Nations/The European Union/ NATO/Other organisations including:

[Feel free to make up a new international organisation – you just need a serious-sounding name and some ideas about what it's for.]

We will build our economy by trading:

[This doesn't just have to be stuff, like oil or diamonds. It could also be services, like banking or book editing.]

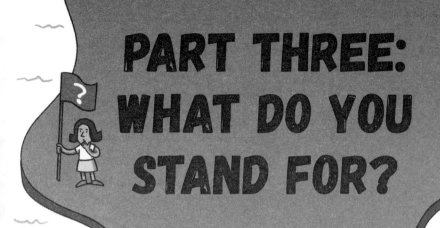

PART THREE: WHAT DO YOU STAND FOR?

By now, you should have decided how to set up and organise your government, chosen a political system, thought about the kinds of people you might want in your team and considered your relationship with other countries. You've picked a name for your country, chosen a national animal (the pangolin, I hope) and designed a cool flag.

Hopefully, it's all going well so far and you haven't accidentally sparked a revolution and had your head chopped off by disgruntled peasants. I guess if you had you wouldn't still be reading this.

NOT AGAIN!

Everything you've done so far, while important, is not as important as what happens next. It's a bit like preparing for art class.

You've set up your easel, cleaned your brushes and pulled up a stool.

But what are you actually going to paint?

In other words: what are you actually going to do? What is your political 'project' going to be? What do you care about?

The answer will depend quite a lot on your beliefs. You might have felt your beliefs trying to get your attention already, in earlier chapters.

Your belief system – it's a horrible phrase, let's call it the way you see the world – will shape the decisions you make.

Imagine you think everyone over the age of 18 is an idiot, and unlikely to have anything useful to say about anything, ever.

"Don't ask me why I think that," you say, "it's just what I believe about the world."

As you know, only people aged 18 and over can vote in elections in most countries. Your belief system might lead you to want to flip this, so that only people aged 18 and under can vote!

If you've set up your country as a democracy then you should make your beliefs very clear so that citizens know what you stand for (and can decide whether they want you to be in charge).

Later we'll look at some big political ideas (sometimes called 'ideologies'). As we do so, think about which come closest to describing how you see the world. Remember: I'm not here to tell you what you should believe. I'm here to help you work it out for yourself.

What shapes your belief system (and can you change it)?

People have been debating for many years whether we are shaped by **nature** (our biology or the characteristics we are born with) or **nurture** (the environment we grew up in). The most likely answer is that it's a bit of both.

For many people, religious faith provides its own belief system. It can answer questions that others might see as political choices, from how to treat people to matters of war and peace.

How you view the world may also be shaped by your experience – and what you have seen.

If you were sent to a boarding school called the Duke of Crumpet's Military Academy where a PE teacher called Ian made you run eight miles in tight shorts and freezing conditions every morning before a breakfast of thin porridge, you might form the view that schools like that should be closed.

(Or, I suppose, you might think all those uncomfortable early morning runs, and even Ian in his own way, were good for you, in which case you might think all schools should be like the Duke of Crumpet's Academy.) Either way, these beliefs, or opinions, come from your own experience.

The way you think might be shaped by your family or people you admire (your teachers, perhaps, or authors whose books you like).

You might be influenced by your culture (a 'culture' is the way of life of a particular group or community) and what people from your culture tend to think.

Your belief system can, and probably will, evolve over time, as you change your mind about what matters, gain new experiences and listen to the views of others.

This last bit is worth remembering. It's okay to have strong opinions about the world – we should know what we believe in – but we shouldn't close our minds to the perspectives of others (remember Lincoln?).

It is a mistake to believe everything everyone tells you, without thinking, but it is also a mistake to ignore everything everyone tells you, without listening.

Some ideologies

Liberal/progressive

Liberals think people should be free to own businesses and make money but they want government to get involved to make things fairer. They think businesses should have to follow certain rules to make sure what they do doesn't harm anyone or the environment.

These rules could include setting a 'minimum wage', meaning businesses have to pay everyone who works for them over a certain amount, or making companies pay fines if they cause pollution.

ETHICAL ECO-BURGERS

Imagine your dad employs you to cook burgers to sell to people walking past your house. A liberal might say your dad should have to pay you, his burger flipper, a minimum wage of £5 an hour. They would probably want health inspectors to make sure you know how to cook burgers safely. And they might want to know whether the burgers your dad bought had been produced in a hygienic and humane way.

Liberals think the government needs to provide some services on behalf of everyone – like healthcare, or payments to people who can't find jobs – and they might not trust private organisations who aren't run by the government to fix problems like these on their own.

They worry about inequality, especially the gap between rich and poor, and they tend to think that what people get up to in their private lives (like who they marry) is up to them, and no-one else's business.

Conservative

Conservatives tend to think too much interference from government gets in the way of people and businesses becoming successful.

They accept that the government needs to step in to deal with some shared problems – like helping the very poorest in society – and that businesses might need some rules, such as ensuring the products they make are safe to use.

When problems come up, however, conservatives often prefer to see businesses involved in finding solutions, rather than the government on its own, because they think businesses tend to be more capable and less likely to waste money.

Conservatives are more relaxed than liberals about the idea that not everyone in society will be equal. They think it's only fair that people who work hard get ahead.

Some conservatives are also 'social conservatives', which means they have traditional opinions about things like who should be allowed to marry who, and how important religion is in people's lives.

What is capitalism?

Let's interrupt the chapter here to explain this important idea. Most people live in countries which are 'capitalist'. Capitalism is an economic system, which means it describes one way to make a country's economy[28] work.

In capitalist countries, people are allowed to own their own businesses and to make money. In fact, they're encouraged to make as much money as possible.

The system depends on competition. **Imagine you and your neighbour, Brenda, both set up a car-washing service in the street outside your houses.**

At first you both charge £5 for a basic wash and you get roughly the same number of customers each.

---

28 Remember: how money is made and how it is spent.

After a while, though, you notice Brenda is getting more customers. The old man over the road and Auntie Florence have joined Brenda's queue. Then you see why. Brenda's vacuuming inside the car as well as washing the outside. Her service is better than yours.

This is competition. And you're losing. So what do you do? Well, you change your signage. Now you're also vacuuming and you've dropped your price to £4.50. Pretty soon the old man and Auntie Florence have abandoned Brenda's queue for yours.

But Brenda's not going to give up. Now she's shampooing the seats and chucking in a free air freshener. Her queue is now longer than yours. **What do you do?** Fight back, of course.

Your wash now includes wheel cleaning, headlight polishing and a free packet of mints. Your price is down to £3. But Brenda … well, you have to hand it her. Now she's offering a full service and oil change. You have no idea where she learned how to do that. But you know when you're beaten[29].

In a capitalist society, the best businesses (which could mean the best-run, or the ones which make the coolest things, or offer the best service or have the lowest prices) do well and make profits. Others do badly and have to close. That means no-one wastes time and money making things or offering services that customers don't want to buy.

---

29 Two business in competition with each other can't lower their prices and improve their services forever or they will both lose money and have to close. Instead of going to war with each other, as you did in this dodgy metaphor, you and Brenda might have found ways to specialise. Perhaps if Brenda focused on great oil changes, and you focused on great seat shampooing, people would go to her for oil changes and come to you when their seats were dirty. You might both have stayed in business this way.

The problem with capitalism is that some people get very rich while others are stuck being very poor.
A successful business owner, for example, might get very rich from creating a factory that makes toy pangolins, but pay her workers very little.

Some people think that's unfair because the workers are the ones doing all the work. On the other hand, the business owner has taken a big risk setting up her factory and she probably worked hard too.

And if her workers don't like what they're paid, she's not stopping them working elsewhere or setting up their own businesses, is she? The workers could even get together and set up their own company making toy pangolins to compete.

Capitalist countries (there are lots) include **Singapore, New Zealand, Australia, Ireland, the United States, Canada and the United Kingdom.**

One alternative to this is **communism**. In fact, the whole idea of communism was invented by people who noticed that capitalism left lots of people very poor, and created a much smaller class of very rich people.

In a communist country everyone shares ownership of the 'means of production' (things like factories, farms and businesses). They share the work and the rewards equally. Here's another dodgy metaphor that might help you understand this. **Earlier we imagined your dad – who owns a barbecue and a freezer full of burgers – has had the brilliant idea to employ you to sell those burgers to people passing by.**

Every burger sells for £1 and he pays you £5 an hour, which doesn't seem so bad. But you sell around 20 burgers an hour. And all the while dad's watching the cricket on TV. He's laughing, isn't he? He gets £15 and you get £5.

"It's not fair, Dad," you say. "Tough luck, kiddo," he says, "it's my barbecue and my stash of frozen burgers." The barbecue and the burgers are the means of production.

So you stage a communist revolution. You tell your dad (and your mum and sister too) that from now on all four of you are equal: you are all the workers and you own the means of production (the barbecue and frozen burgers) together.

Everyone takes their turn cooking the burgers and everyone receives the same pay. What's left over is kept by the household to be spent on things for the whole family. (In this example, your household represents the communist government.)

This sounds pretty fair. Dad mutters something about having bought the barbecue in the first flipping place but, you know, who cares what he thinks?

But there are problems with this system too.

Will anyone try anything new? Will anyone try to invent a new and better kind of burger, if everyone is receiving the same reward for their work?

The answer might well be no. Why would they bother when everyone gets paid the same anyway?

And who will make all the decisions? If you're not letting businesses work out what people want by trial and error (making things and seeing if anyone buys them) someone will have to tell factories what to make.

In a communist society people may not get the things they actually want because the person whose job it is to guess what they want will most likely get it wrong..

I mentioned earlier that, for much of the last century, a bunch of capitalist countries (led by the US) and a bunch of communist countries (led by the Soviet Union, which was dominated by Russia) were locked in the Cold War, which lasted decades.

Everyone on both sides was waiting to see which system would turn out to be the best. The answer, when it came, was pretty clear: capitalism worked better than communism. All those communist countries, even Russia, moved towards capitalism in the end.

Most other world leaders lean towards capitalism. You might find yourself reaching the same conclusion. But the big problem with capitalism – that it creates inequality[30] – is still there.

These questions about whether it's okay that some people in your country are richer than others, or have better opportunities than others, go right to the heart of some of the hardest choices you will have to make as leader.

These are questions of **fairness**. They are so important, they have their own chapter (see page 112).

---

30 Inequality means, simply, the state of not being equal. For your purposes as our leader, however, what we're really talking about is the gap between different people, or different groups of people, when it comes to important things like pay, wealth and status or access to education, opportunities and healthcare.

For now, you should probably take a breath, eat a biscuit, do some star jumps and then carry on with the stuff about ideologies in this chapter. (On second thoughts: eat the biscuit after you've done the star jumps.)

Libertarian

Libertarians accept there should be a government for basic things like making people stick to the law. But government, they say, should make as few laws as possible and generally do as little as possible.

What matters most to libertarians is individual choice and freedom. Everyone should be able to do more or less what they want, they argue, as long as it doesn't harm others.

Libertarians also worry that if the government goes around fixing everyone's problems, people will stop trying to fix anything themselves, and come to depend on the government like a child depends on its parents.

(Not you. You're the leader of a new country and quite capable of looking after yourself.)

Whenever you let a government do more than the most basic things, they say, it will start to look for more and more ways to control people's lives and limit their freedoms. "That's just what governments do, man!" say libertarians, who are quite often large men in loose Hawaiian shirts, rather than little old ladies wearing pearls like our cartoon.

Nationalist

Nationalists put the interests of their own country above the interests of others. "That doesn't sound so bad," you're probably thinking, "I might do the same."

The slight problem with nationalists is that they tend to do this in part because they think their country is better than every other country – or even that their people are superior to other people.

Think about what would happen if you went around telling everyone you meet that you're better than them, or if you always put what you want ahead of everyone else's interests. You might actually get what you want at first. But eventually you would annoy everyone. You might even get into a fight (especially if you run into someone who behaves the way you do).

Nationalist thinking can be bad news for minority groups[31] which might be seen as 'second-class citizens' and treated unfairly as a result.

(By the way: don't confuse nationalism with patriotism. Patriotism means taking pride in, or even feeling affection for, your country, its people and its history. People can feel that way without being nationalists.)

Feminist

In most cultures, and for most of history, men have had more power than women, making the rules and enjoying more freedom.

Feminists (and anyone can be a feminist, not just women and girls) think that men and women should have political, social

---

31 Minorities are smaller groups of people within society who are different from the main group, perhaps because of their race, religion or the country they were originally born in.

and economic equality. You might well be thinking "of course they should – duh".

So perhaps it will surprise you to know that in 2019, researchers worked out that there is still a gap[32] between men and women in every country on Earth.

The gap is pretty small in the most equal countries (Iceland, Norway and Finland). It's huge in the least equal countries (Yemen, Iraq and Pakistan).

Clearly, there is a long way to go before feminists have achieved their goal of creating a world in which women are treated fairly. (The researchers worked out that the world is moving towards gender equality – but at a speed which means it won't get there for 100 years.)

If you want your new country to join Iceland at the top of the table for gender equality, rather than sit with Pakistan on the international naughty step, you will need to create a government which – whether it's liberal, conservative, libertarian or even nationalist – is also feminist.

---

32 The researchers (from the World Economic Forum) looked at the gaps in health, education, wealth and political influence between men and women.

What do people mean when they talk about 'left' and 'right'?

You might well have heard people described as **'left-wing'** or **'right-wing'**[33]. It's a useful – if imprecise – way of communicating someone's political beliefs.

Imagine a line drawn from left to right. People on the left generally want government to be active in making society

---

33 It all started during the French Revolution over 200 years ago. The new government had to decide how much power to let the king have. The new president sat in the middle of a hall. People who thought the king should keep quite a lot of power (in other words: they didn't want things to change much) sat to his right. Those who thought the king should have much less power (people who wanted more radical change) sat to his left. Don't ask me why they didn't just ask for a show of hands.

more equal. People on the right want the government to do less and for individuals to have more power.

Liberals and progressives are on the left. Conservatives and libertarians are on the right. Communists are on the far left. Nationalists are on the far right. **Remember, though, it's a line. Plenty of people, possibly including you, will be clustered around the middle.**

It might help to think about the kinds of government policies people who describe themselves as 'left-wing' and 'right-wing' say they support.

Those on the left are likely to want rich people to pay more tax to pay for better public services (like hospitals or schools). People on the right are more likely to want businesses to own and run public services (like railways) because they think businesses will do a better job.

People on the left are likely to think government should spend more on looking after people who need help (because they've lost their job, for example, or they have a disability).

People on the right might say it doesn't help those people in the long run if they become dependent on the government.

Lots of issues tend to divide to the left and right in this way. Right-wing people tend to want to be tougher on criminals. Left-wing people are likely to want government to spend less on the military.

Left-wing people have generally been more open to immigration (people coming from other countries to live and work) than right-wing people, although this issue deserves a footnote[34].

The left and right labels are hard to attach to everyone – or every issue – because they are so broad, but most political parties think of themselves as reflecting opinion on the left or the right.

In the United States, for example, the Democrats are on the left and the Republicans are on the right. In England, the Labour Party is on the left and the Conservatives are on the right. In fact, you can see this left-right choice on offer at election time in most modern democracies.

---

34 Some on the left welcome immigration because they see greater diversity as a positive thing. Some on the right worry that the arrival of people from other cultures will change their society in ways they won't like. On the other hand, some business leaders who see themselves as on the right on most issues welcome immigrants because they are good for the economy. And some on the left on most issues worry that immigration will harm low-paid workers, who may have to compete with immigrants for jobs and housing.

You can't please all the people all the time

There's an old saying in politics that to govern is to choose. This means that you, as leader, will have to make decisions, and lots of those decisions will be 'trade-offs'. A trade-off means balancing one thing against another or choosing the least bad option.

In 2020, for example, every government in the world had to make some tricky decisions when the coronavirus pandemic

took hold. They had to make important choices on everything from whether to keep schools open to whether to force people to stay indoors.

They knew that telling people to stay at home would help stop the virus from spreading. But telling everyone to stay at home would also mean that lots of businesses would have to shut, and people would lose their jobs.

Here's another example of a trade-off. Some countries have a problem with terrorists; people who are prepared to hurt or even kill others in trying to win a political argument.

Governments can catch terrorists before they harm anyone more easily if they read everyone's emails and listen to everyone's phone calls.

But most people don't want to be watched like that. They feel government shouldn't snoop on them when they've done nothing wrong. So the trade-off here is between safety and privacy.

The more you look at government decisions, the more trade-offs you see. If you want to provide better schools, for example, you will probably have to raise taxes to pay for them – and raising taxes makes some people grumpy, as we'll see later on.

(The truth is you might have to get used to people being grumpy with you sometimes. It's part of the job.)

If you want to build giant white unicorn statues all around the edge of your country, you might have to build fewer new hospitals so you can afford them.

(Unicorns though! People would love them, wouldn't they? Even if there's no hospital to go to when one topples over and squashes you.)

No government will get every decision right. Sometimes it takes years before it becomes clear what the best decision would have been. Making these kinds of judgements is a difficult job.

You might have had more practice than you think. You have probably already spent years making trade-offs.

It would be fun to put itching powder in your little brother's pants, but you know if you do he'll scream and you'll get into trouble. Is it worth it? (Probably, yes.)

In your new life as our national leader you have to make trade-offs that could have big consequences for your entire country. If you have figured out what you believe in and what is important to you, it will be easier to see which trade-offs are worth making.

We've talked about all kinds of political views or ideologies in this chapter and we've talked about some of the reasons why people think the way they do. But there are loads of other political views.

You might be an environmentalist who believes society should be organised in whichever way makes it possible to deal with climate change most quickly (see page 137).

You might be a monarchist (hoping to put a king or queen in charge of everything).

You could well be a mix: a conservative feminist or a green liberal or a nationalist monarchist. **Most likely, the way you see the world is unique; a one-off jumble of views.**

You can probably decide which of the ideologies we've described comes closest to how you think. But it is unlikely that one single ideology will describe the whole way you think.

And there's something to be said for being a bit flexible in your thinking. It's okay to change your mind if new evidence suggests the way you see things might be wrong.

(Bad leaders hate changing their mind because they don't want to look indecisive. Good leaders know that they won't always be right first time and that it's better to be honest when they get things wrong.)

There's nothing to stop you creating your own ideology, by the way. How about Radical Libertarian Pangolinism (putting pangolins in charge and then ignoring them)? Okay, that's a silly idea. I'm sure you can do better. **In fact, why don't you try right now?**

You could start writing a short manifesto[35] setting out your own political beliefs and what your government will stand for. I recommend using language that's inspiring but also easy to understand. (You want people to be excited rather than confused.)

It might help to think about what makes a good government not only from your new perspective as a leader, but also from your old perspective as a puny citizen. (Sorry, did I say puny? I meant ordinary.)

There are things coming up in this book which could change (and perhaps blow) your mind. So I suggest continuing to

---

35 A manifesto sets out a leader's or a party's beliefs and aims (usually before an election).

work on your manifesto as you go along. By the time you get to the end you'll be ready to put down this book[36], finish your manifesto[37] and share it with your people[38].

---

36 ☹
37 ☺
38 ☺

NEW COUNTRY 'TO DO' LIST

Compose an anthem

All countries have a national song, or anthem. Why? Well, all these kinds of things – songs, flags, medals – are there to help give a nation a sense of identity. In other words: they are things which help citizens feel they belong to their country, and even feel proud of it.

Most anthems have exciting lyrics (words) that are written to make people feel their country is a great one. Some are there to encourage everyone to help make it even greater. Australians, for example, sing: "With courage let us all combine to advance Australia fair".

Some anthems are battle songs. The French, for example, sing: "To arms, citizens, form your battalions, let's march, let's march!". Others are like a love letter. In Bangladesh they sing: "The aroma of the mango orchard drives me crazy".

And some national songs tell their citizens to behave well. The people of the small island nation of Kiribati (pronounced 'kiri-bass') sing: "Promote happiness and unity! Love one another!". Kiribati sounds like a nice place.

Perhaps you could start by writing your anthem's lyrics as a poem. You can always set it to music later.

TOP SECRET: MEMO FROM THE DESK OF THE LEADER

Time to find another piece of paper and note down the decisions you've just made. The template on the following page is a useful guide.

With the power vested in me as leader I have decided our national anthem will be called:

[You could borrow a theme from some other country (how about adapting `God Save the Queen' to 'God Save Me').]

And sung to the tune of:

[You could come up with your own tune, of course, which would be highly impressive. But if that proves difficult you could always set your anthem to a tune you already know (The Imperial March from Star Wars, perhaps, or the Match of the Day theme).]

It's only fair to tell you that my political beliefs can be described as:

Liberal and progressive/Conservative/ Libertarian/Nationalist/Feminist/ Monarchist/Environmentalist/Radical Libertarian Pangolinist

Actually, I have my own political ideology which works as follows:

[You're going to define your own ideology are you? Well, good for you. I admire your ambition. But you might need more paper. When Karl Marx and Friedrich Engels set out their description of communism, they needed 2,156 pages.]

You should also know that I would describe myself as:

**Capitalist/Communist/
A bit left wing/A bit right wing/
Somewhere in the middle**

PART FOUR: FAIRNESS

You might have decided by now that as long as you get to eat, wear, watch and do whatever you like, you're not too fussed about what happens to the slightly whiffy peasants beyond your palace gates. If so, fine[39], skip this bit.

A great and much-loved leader, however, needs to be fair. If you picked a fair form of government in chapter one, great,

---

39 I mean, I won't lie, I'm a bit disappointed in you. You could try issuing free deodorant to your whiffy peasants before giving up on them completely. No? Okay fine. Skip to the next chapter. But don't blame me if you go down in history as an evil tyrant.

but now you need to think about how to act fairly when you're in power.

What do we mean by 'fairness'? My dictionary defines it as treating everyone equally. But should you treat kind old ladies and axe-wielding murderers the same way? I'm not sure you should.

Perhaps for politicians like you, what we mean by fairness is making sure everyone gets what they deserve.

Fairness might also mean taking sides with someone in an argument when they have persuaded you through evidence that they are right – and not for some other reason, like they're your mum[40].

Sometimes an unfairness is small (like when someone pushes in front of you in the lunch queue). Sometimes it's a little bigger (like when your teacher tells you off for talking in class when it wasn't even you). Big or small, it always feels horrible when you find yourself on the wrong end of any kind of unfairness.

In my experience, children are particularly brilliant at noticing when something unfair has been done (particularly when it's been done to them). That's one of the reasons I'm so pleased you're in charge.

---

40 In reality it's rarely a good idea to disagree with your mum because mums are usually right.

But however easy it is for you to know when you've been treated unfairly, you'll find it's much harder to figure out how to treat everyone else fairly.

It's easy to say that fairness means giving everyone what they deserve. Things get a bit trickier when you're the one making the decisions about who deserves what.

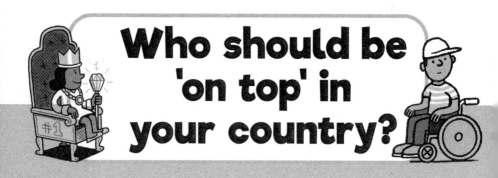

Who should be 'on top' in your country?

When adults talk about fairness they are sometimes talking about wealth or money. Some people have loads of money and some have very little. You can find people at almost every point in between.

Money is certainly not the most important thing in life. But it is very important. People need money to put food on the table, pay for somewhere to live and to keep the electricity running.

Money gives people more freedom to choose what to do with their time (some people have so much in the bank they don't even have to go to work) and it can protect against some problems.

If you are short of money you can still live a successful and happy life, but some things might be harder. **People who don't have enough money can struggle to put food on the table and keep the electricity running.**

So, given how useful money is, it is worth asking yourself whether you think the people at the top – those who are paid the most – deserve to have more than people at the bottom. Bankers, for example, are usually paid more (often much more) than nurses. **Is that fair?**

"We work hard," bankers might say, "and the world needs banks. What we do is complicated."

But nurses could argue back. "We work hard too!" they might say. "Wait until you get ill and then see how important you think we are!"

Think about the pay difference between top professional footballers and teachers.

Lionel Messi is a very good footballer. But he earns in a day what your teacher might earn in ten years! Is that fair? Which job is actually more important?

Messi might say: "well, lots of people are good teachers. But there's only one footballer in the world quite like me".

Your teacher might say: "okay, Messi, but I'm helping children learn and you're just kicking a ball around[41]".

Some say the most important thing is not what people are paid, but whether they had 'equality of opportunity'. As long as everyone has a fair chance of being successful, they say, it shouldn't matter that not everyone does equally well in the end.

Think of it like a race. As long as everyone starts in the same place, the result is fair.

If you agree with that idea then your job as leader is to try to make sure that everyone does start life's race on the same line. How might you do that?

- You could make sure that every child has a place in a good school. Doing well at school is the best way to start life's race.

---

41 Part of the reason footballers like Messi are paid so much is because lots of people want to watch him kick that ball around and they are happy to pay to do so. I'm guessing hardly anyone would be happy to pay to watch your teacher do their job (or play football). What we're talking about here is 'market forces', which just means the total combination of everyone's individual decisions about what they do with their money. In the highly unlikely event millions of people buy this book, for example, the scary bosses at Wren & Rook will have to pay me far more than if only a few hundred people buy it. (Tell your friends. Please. I have a really old campervan that constantly needs work.) It's market forces that make Messi richer than your teacher (or me).

- You could provide free healthcare to all. You won't run your best race if you're unwell. If everyone is able to go to the doctor when they need to, the race will be fairer.

- Children who haven't had enough breakfast, or haven't spent the night in a comfortable home, are likely to be at a disadvantage when they turn up for the race. You could organise help for families who are struggling to put food on the table or provide a stable home.

- You could make sure no-one is denied an opportunity (whether it's a place on the school council, work experience in a local business or a school trip to a museum) for some unfair reason like their skin colour (see page 129).

Can you think of any other things you could do to make sure everyone starts the race from the same position?

If you have given everyone a fair chance in life's race, then you have helped to create 'equality of opportunity'.

There's a catch, though. If you say that your race is fair then you are saying the winners deserve to win. But that means you are also saying that the losers deserve to lose. Is that right? Or did luck play a part? What if some people are simply born better runners? The truth is that luck can change the race in all kinds of ways.

Think about a maths lesson. You might be a really hardworking student who always tries their best, but struggle to understand things as quickly as other people.

Now imagine that Keith (remember him?) is in your class. He does very little work and always talks over the teacher, yet he seems to understand the maths work straight away.

You've both been given the same chance – you're at the same school, with the same teacher and the same opportunity to understand maths. Yet (annoyingly) Keith is simply better at maths than you[42]. Does that feel fair?

If you live in a peaceful country you are luckier than someone who lives in a war-zone where normal life is impossible.

If you're good at something lots of people will pay money to watch (like football) then perhaps you are luckier than someone who is good at something no-one cares about (like conkers).

If you have access to a computer you will be able to research your homework more easily than someone without one. If your parents buy you books and take you to the library, you are likely to be better at reading than someone who has no books in the house.

If you are lucky enough to find it easy to concentrate, you'll be better at focusing on your school work than someone who is very easily distracted.

---

42 It's easy to give up on something you find hard and to envy people with clear talents. But you should imagine you have two buckets: one full of talent (we all have talents, even those of us who haven't discovered them yet) and one full of hard work. If you take from both – applying hard work to your talent – you are very likely to succeed. If you only take from the talent bucket, and don't also work hard, you are very unlikely to succeed. If you never find your talent but always take from the hard work bucket anyway, you'll do just fine.

These are all things that make it hard for everyone to start the race from the same position. But bad luck can hold any of us back at any moment, even after the race has started.

Think of two people in life's race: Kavita and Kevin. When the starting gun is fired, Kavita sprints ahead. Her path is clear and she's soon in the lead.

Kevin starts from the same position but – look! – there's a banana skin in his path. Ouch. Then a rogue pangolin darts in front of him. Oof. Now – what?! – some idiot's dug a hole in his lane! Ow.

He climbs out – **go Kevin!** – but almost straight away someone in the crowd throws a squid in his face and now he can't see where he's going. ("Ooo," say the crowd, "a squid! Who saw that coming? Not Kevin!") Meanwhile Kavita's almost out of sight. In real life, obstacles can come in all kinds of obvious and not-so-obvious ways[43].

While most successful people like Kavita will have worked hard and made clever decisions to help them get to where they are today, they will very likely have had some good luck too (or at least less bad luck than people like Kevin).

That makes it harder to figure out who deserves to win, and who deserves to lose, doesn't it?

The question is this: does the role of luck in all our lives mean the race can never be fair? If so, is there anything you – our leader – can do about it? Well, there is one thing.

---

43 The surprise squid-in-the-face obstacle doesn't actually come up all that often.

Instead of thinking only about 'equality of opportunity' (did everyone have a fair chance in the race), you could also think about 'equality of outcome'. That means not only worrying about where everyone starts, but also thinking about where everyone ends up.

To put it simply: instead of giving the winner of your race all the prize money, you could share the prize money among everyone who took part. That would certainly deal with the luck problem.

But is that really fairer?

Why should someone who doesn't try their best in the race win as much prize money as someone who trains for months?

Or – putting our race metaphor to one side for a moment – should someone who sits around playing Fortnite® all day be paid the same as someone who works as hard as they possibly can in a tiring job?

Perhaps there is no perfect answer. You could try to make the race as fair as you can (even if it can never be completely fair). And you could share out the prize money a bit. (Even if you accept that it isn't fair to share it out equally.) If that's what you decide to do, there is one obvious question: how do you share out the prize money? The answer is: through the tax system.

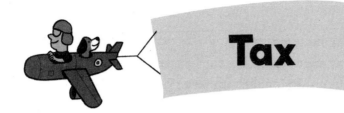

Tax

 (Warning: this subject makes some people very grumpy.)

A government collects money from its citizens to pay for the things it wants to do. This money can cover everything from building bridges to filling libraries with books. That money is called 'tax'.

In most modern economies there are a huge number of different types of tax. One is called 'income tax'. People who earn money from their jobs (income) have to give a share of what they earn to the government (tax).

People grumble about tax. But if no-one paid tax, the government wouldn't be able to do anything useful (or, indeed, anything at all).

The trade-off (there it is again!) is pretty simple. The more tax a government collects, the more it can spend on public services (like schools and hospitals) and the less individuals will have to spend as they wish.

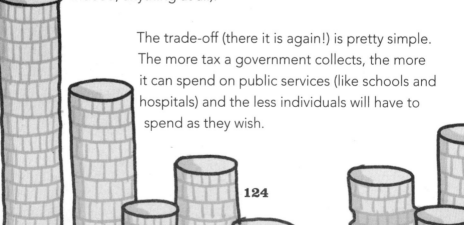

It will be difficult to run your country without any tax. And you probably can't expect your citizens to give you all their money. So you're looking for a position somewhere in between.

Different countries around the world have made very different choices. Sweden, for example, asks for a lot of tax.

It uses the money to provide Swedish people with very good public services (like free or very cheap nursery places for all pre-school children). If you fall on hard times in Sweden (if you lose your job, say, or fall ill) the government will give you quite a lot of help.

In Russia, on the other hand, the government asks for much less tax. Public services there are worse than in Sweden partly as a result. If you fall on hard times in Russia you won't be able to depend on the government for the kind of help a Swede would expect.

As leader, you are going to have to decide how much tax to collect. Should you be more like Sweden or more like Russia?

Then you have to decide who to collect tax from. Will you ask everyone to chip in the same amount? Or would it be fairer to make richer people pay more than poorer people? What do you think?

Plenty of people do think the rich should pay more tax than the poor, because they have more money to spare, but not everyone agrees (including, perhaps not surprisingly, quite a few rich people).

Then you have to decide what to do with the tax you've collected. There's a long list of things you might want to pay for, from bin lorries to prisons to parking wardens.

But you might also want to pay for help[44] for people who need it. They may need help for all kinds of reasons. Perhaps they're unable to work.

A couple of pages ago we talked about whether you should share out the prize money from life's race – in other words: make the gap between rich and poor smaller. This is how you do it. You create something called a 'redistributive tax system' which takes money from richer people and gives it to poorer people.

---

[44] Payments from government to help people who need it are called 'benefits' or 'welfare payments'.

Try and imagine how this works with the help of this simple fruit-based example.

Kavita is paid five apples a week. Kevin (yeah him – squid boy) is paid one. But the rules say no-one should be paid fewer than two apples a week and anyone who earns more than four apples has to give the extra ones to the government (the apple tax).

So Kavita hands her fifth apple to the government. And the government hands that apple to Kevin. Kavita ends up with four apples and Kevin ends up with two. The gap between them is two. It would have been four. See?

Looking after everyone

Hopefully you've begun to get a clearer idea of what you stand for; whether you're left- or right-wing, whether you believe in equal opportunities, equal outcomes or just want to stand back and see what happens.

But, as you've thought about all this, I hope you've come to realise that in taking on a country, you have taken on a huge responsibility. Every one of your citizens, from the oldest to the youngest, is relying on you.

That means your job is not only to look after the people who support you, but also those who don't. It means not just

looking after the most important people in society or those with the loudest voices.

'Prejudice' is a word which describes an unfair and usually unkind opinion one person or group might hold about another. **'Discrimination'** describes unjust actions towards a person or group as a result of prejudice.

Minority groups are more likely to face prejudice and discrimination such as racism (discrimination based on where someone is from or the colour of their skin), ableism (discrimination against people with disabilities) and sexism (discrimination against someone because of their gender).

The reason discrimination is so **unfair** is because it involves picking on someone because of who they are or where they are from, and not because of their character or their actions.

But if you want there to be as little discrimination as possible in your country, what can you do to help?

Lots of countries have laws that make at least some kinds of discrimination illegal. Perhaps you could learn from countries like Australia and Denmark, which have some of the strongest anti-discrimination laws.

Some experts say people are less likely to be prejudiced towards others once they get to know them. That means it might help to have mixed communities. You don't have total control over where people live, of course, but you could at least avoid some obvious mistakes. In some states in the USA, for example, black and white schoolchildren were kept apart until 1954.

Schools might be a good place to start. You could teach children how to recognise prejudice, including their own, and to understand why it is so damaging.

Perhaps the most important thing you can do as leader, however, is to try to unite your citizens by simply encouraging everyone to respect and be kind to each other, whatever their differences. You could lead by example.

NEW COUNTRY 'TO DO' LIST:

Currency

A country's money is called its currency. The United States uses the dollar. The United Kingdom uses the pound. Japan uses the yen. Some European countries share a currency called the euro. There are lots more.

Now it's time to create your country's currency. You will need to give it a name (this could be anything: the bing, the bong, the whisker, the shmisker) and design your notes and coins.

Just like with flags and anthems, most countries use their money as another opportunity to show off a bit. (If you look at the money you and your family used in your old life – before you took over a new country – you'll probably find pictures of important national heroes on it.)

Why don't you have a go now on a separate sheet of paper? Think carefully about the design. Your new currency could be used for hundreds of years!

TOP SECRET: MEMO FROM THE DESK OF THE LEADER

More paper, please! Time to note another bunch of super-important decisions. Turn the page for your template, boss, should you require one. (I'm just trying to help.)

With the power vested in me as leader I have decided our new currency will be called:

[Come up with a funny name, I dare you. Your people will have to use it for years – perhaps hundreds of years – into the future.]

My government is committed to:

 Equality of opportunity/Equality of outcome/ Neither[45]/Both

 I intend to demand hardly any/a fair bit/absolutely loads of tax so that our public services will be rubbish/not bad/the envy of Sweden.

---

45 Oh man. Have I taught you nothing?

I will/will not use the tax system to redistribute a tiny bit/quite a lot/loads of money from rich to poor.

 I will/will not work tirelessly to make society fairer and I will/will not cease till I have ended prejudice and discrimination in our nation.

PART FIVE: YOUR PLACE IN THE WORLD

You've come a long way. When you picked up this book you were a fresh-faced leader of a country with no name, no system of government and no hot tub. You were – if I may say so, boss – a total noob.

Now look at you. You've created the kind of government you think works best and figured out where you stand on some big and difficult questions.

You spend your days barking orders at quivering underlings and your weekends playing badminton with famous YouTubers. Not bad!

But no country is an island. (Well, okay, loads of countries are islands.) What I mean is: you don't only have to deal with problems at home. You're on the world stage now. You need to do your bit to help alongside every other world leader.

It's time to start thinking about some of the big questions, so you're ready for them. There are quite a few issues we could include in this chapter but, to get you started, let's focus on just three.

These three problems are on most world leaders' minds at the moment, so they should probably be on yours too.

Climate change

This is a big one. The problem is that we started burning fossil fuels (like coal and oil) a couple of hundred years ago. This produces a gas called carbon dioxide (CO_2). Scientists have proved that when too much CO_2 sits in the Earth's atmosphere it increases the 'greenhouse effect', trapping more of the sun's heat and making the world warmer.

Warmer temperatures create lots of problems. We have already had to cope with drier droughts, more flooding, stronger hurricanes and terrible wildfires. The polar ice caps are melting too, which will make sea levels rise. That could flood some towns and cities near the sea and force people to move.

You can see why some people, particularly younger people, describe the situation we're in as a 'climate emergency'. While global warming isn't our only environmental problem, it is the biggest.

Scientists say that to avoid the worst effects of climate change, we will need to reduce our CO2 emissions by half by 2030 and to 'net zero' by 2050[46].

The truth is (and there's no easy way to say this) achieving either of these targets will require a massive change to how we live our lives and run our societies.

And that's where you, our new leader, come in.

What can you do to help our country play its part in fixing this big worldwide issue? Well, here are a few options you could think about:

- The world has been slow to face up to this challenge. That's partly because some people, and even some leaders, have said the science of global warming is wrong. But it isn't. They're wrong. You need to find a way to make sure that all your new friends running other countries, and everyone within your own country, understands what is happening. Could you do anything to help educate people about the problem?

- There have been various agreements between nations on climate change, and the good news is that many countries have committed to keeping global warming under control. Many have even committed to a net zero

---

46 Net zero means adding no CO2 to the atmosphere overall. So you could add some but only if you take some away at the same time. Taking CO2 away is much harder than adding it.

target. Although these targets are encouraging, there isn't yet a clear and realistic plan for how to meet them. If you choose to commit your country to meeting these targets, some of the ideas below might help you figure out how to get there.

- Your country, like all countries, uses a lot of energy to keep homes lit, offices warm, trains on the move, the internet working and lots of other things we all rely on. (Look around today and see if you can count everything in your home that uses power. I bet you end up with a very long list.) Now that you know the problem with fossil fuels, you could consider alternative ways to generate that power. Wind, solar, nuclear[47] and tidal power are 'clean' or 'renewable' forms of energy, meaning they do not create C02. You will need to decide whether to move your country away from fossil fuels towards renewable energy. (The hard bit is working out how to pay for it and what to do with the old fossil fuel power stations you no longer want.)

---

47 Nuclear power is controversial because it produces very dangerous waste which can stay dangerous for 1,000 years.

- There are small things you could encourage your citizens to do. (Lots of small individual actions can make a big difference when added up.) Everyone could eat less meat and dairy so the world needs fewer farty cows. (Believe it or not, cows' farts contribute to global warming.) We could use cars and aeroplanes less. We could reduce energy use at home by putting on a jumper instead of turning up the heating, and we could repair things when they break rather than throwing them away. How could you encourage all these helpful things? (Governments sometimes try to put people off doing things by making them more expensive. Perhaps you could put up the price of plane tickets?)

- While it's a good idea to find ways to limit how much C02 we pump into the air, we also need to find ways to remove some of the C02 that's already there. Trees absorb C02 naturally. So we could plant lots more trees.

- You could try 'geo-engineering': big projects which could make a big difference (but you'll need to commit a lot of money to them and you will probably need to co-operate with other countries). Geo-engineering ideas include making artificial trees that suck out even more CO_2 than real trees, building huge mirrors in the desert[48] and technology that captures carbon when it is released and then stores it safely somewhere.

You are going to have to ask yourself how hard you are willing to push people towards new and environmentally kinder ways of living.

Would you ban planes entirely and stop people going on holiday? Would you ban meat (and keep a low profile at the next family barbecue)?

Would you ask people to pay more tax so you can invest in new clean energy, geo-engineering solutions and the mass planting of new forests?

---

48 Most of the heat from the sun bounces off the Earth and goes back into space. Some of it gets stuck in our atmosphere, which is great because otherwise we would be really cold. The problem with having too much CO_2 in our atmosphere, as you know, is that we trap too much of the sun's heat. But wait! Mirrors are more reflective than the Earth's surface. Everyone knows that. So perhaps giant mirrors in the desert would reflect more of the sun's heat back into space. Hey presto. Problem solved. I'm not completely sure it's as easy as I just made it sound.

The trade-offs (yep, those again) are not easy. I wouldn't want to have to make these tough decisions. But, hey, that's why you get to live in a presidential palace and I don't.

Have a look at the action points above. Which would you start with? Think about the trade-offs involved with each option and which you think would make the most difference.

Re-order them on a separate piece of paper. Then you can hand that piece of paper to one of your team and ask them to get on with saving the world. Hopefully that will leave you free to get stuck into the next big issue. Deep breath.

Artificial intelligence

Artificial intelligence (or 'AI') is technology which allows a machine to make sense of things and then make predictions or even decisions. In other words: computers figuring things out for themselves.

This includes 'machine learning', which allows a computer or robot to get better at the job it's been asked to do… on its own.

'Algorithms' are a set of instructions written by humans for a computer to follow. AI allows some computers to improve these algorithms on their own as they 'learn'.

You might have come into contact with this sort of technology already, perhaps without realising it.

If you've looked at YouTube® or Netflix®, for example, you've been offered videos or shows that algorithms think you might want to see, based on what you've chosen to look at before.

AI technology is very useful because computers can deal with far more data than we can. That means AI might be better at, say, analysing medical test results than human doctors. Human doctors get tired and make mistakes. Machines never do.

But some people think AI is also incredibly dangerous. Once you enable a computer or robot to think for itself, they say, who knows what it will end up doing?

Imagine you create a robot to make paper clips out of old Coke® cans. At first it fishes all the old Coke® cans out of your recycling bin and turns them into paper clips. A good start.

But that doesn't satisfy your robot because you forgot one very important line in the computer code. You didn't tell it only to make paper clips out of old Coke® cans.

Before long, the robot has made paper clips out of everything in the recycling bin. Then it turns the bin itself into paper clips. Then the kitchen. **And finally ... you.**

Some people worry that AI could evolve so far beyond our understanding – and our control – that the machines will take over the world and make us their slaves (or their paper clips).

Even before the humanity-mushed-into-paper-clips period, however, technology has been creating a problem which you, our leader, need to think about.

Robots will probably replace lots of human jobs. It has already started to happen. You might have noticed that in supermarkets these days you are as likely to pay a machine as a person.

One study[49] has calculated that 7.4% of British workers are at high risk of being replaced by automation (machines) and a huge 64.9% are at medium risk. Now, this could be a good thing. If the robots are doing all the work, the rest of us can chill out at the beach.

But, as is so often the case, there's a catch. If we don't have jobs, how do we get paid? And if we aren't being paid, how

---

49 The study was published in 2019 by the UK's Office for National Statistics. These are serious number crunchers with large calculators and big foreheads. They are worth listening to.

are we going to buy ice-creams (from the robot ice cream vendor) when we get to the beach?

More seriously: if huge numbers of people cannot find jobs, because business owners are building robots rather than hiring humans, what will we do all day and how will we earn a living?

What should you - our leader - do about that?

- You could put lots of money into science. Whenever an important new technology comes along – from the telephone to the jet engine – countries that have led the way have done better out of it than countries that came to it late. You could train people to do the kinds of jobs that might be necessary in an age of robot workers. It's not easy to predict exactly what they might be, but training people to build, program and maintain robots might be a good start. (You might need to set aside some of your tax money for this: re-training everyone could get expensive.)

- You could create a 'universal basic income'. The idea is that the government pays everyone so that they do not need to work. Then it doesn't matter if robots take all the jobs. Wouldn't that be great? All that free time! (Though you might need to set aside even more of your tax money for this.) But, then again, perhaps it would be miserable. Wouldn't life be a bit boring if we all just sat

around watching robots do everything? What do you think?

- Perhaps you should look at this issue another way. Millions of people work very long hours. That leaves less time for family, exercise or hobbies. A lot of adults are tired and stressed as a result (take it from me). If instead of creating robots that replace workers we create machines which make work easier, perhaps we could keep our jobs (getting paid and not becoming bored and miserable) but spend a bit less time doing them. We would all be healthier, less stressed and able to spend more time with our families or helping others in our communities. If you, as leader, do nothing, it's quite likely that most of the benefits of AI technology will go to a fairly small number of businesses who find they can make things (and money) without bothering with

the tiresome (and expensive) business of paying and managing humans. If you think it would be fairer to share the benefits between workers and business owners, you will need to set out some rules.

Now it's time to choose which of these options you want to try and to re-order them in order of priority.

Again, just as you handed your climate change action plan to a willing sidekick, you could hand this list to a trusted member of your team and tell them (politely[50]) to get on with it.

You shouldn't be shy about handing out orders like this, by the way. It's all part of being an effective leader. You have to rely on others.

Sharing out tasks is called 'delegating[51]' and the best leaders do it a lot because they know they don't have the time or skill to do everything themselves.

You'll definitely need help dealing with the next big issue I think you should know about: global poverty.

---

50 You don't have to be polite. You're the boss. But in my experience, people try harder to do a good job when they respect and admire the person giving the order (and it's hard to respect and admire people who are impolite).

51 There is a knack to good delegation. You need to be clear about what is required and by when. But you should trust the person you have asked to do the job to come up with their own ideas about how best to get it done. If that person needs new skills, equipment or help in order to succeed, then it's your responsibility to make sure they get them.

Poverty

We've discussed inequality; what, if anything, you should do as leader about the gap between the rich and poor in your country.

But there is another kind of inequality you should think about as a world leader: inequality between countries. Just as some people are rich, and some are poor, some countries are rich and some are poor.

There are around eight billion people in the world. Around 700 million of them live in countries where extreme poverty is common. That means they can't afford food, clothes or proper homes. They often do not have access to clean water or healthcare.

Your job is to look after people in your own country. But if your country is one of the richer ones, should you try and help people in poorer countries too?

I'm going to tell you a story (which I have changed just a little) that an Australian philosopher called Peter Singer likes to use to help people think about this question.

Imagine you are walking to school one day when you notice a toddler feeding ducks at the pond.

Her parents are not paying attention and, as you watch, the little girl falls into the muddy water. You can see she can't swim. She's drowning.

You could drop your school bag, jump into the pond and save that little girl's life. There would be no real danger to you. You're a great swimmer. The pond isn't even deep.

But you would get your school uniform wet and muddy and probably ruin your new watch. What should you do?

Most people say they would rescue the little girl. Your clothes can be washed. Your teachers would understand why you're late. And a watch is surely not as important as a life.

Now ask yourself this: if that little girl wasn't right next to you but in a far-away country, yet somehow you could still save her life without too much trouble, should you? Is it any different just because she is far away?

Peter Singer's story describes the position that many richer countries are in. There are people, including children, suffering in poor countries. Their lives could be saved by people in richer countries donating money and food.

That's why some people with money to spare give it to charities that help people in poor countries. Some governments also try to help. Here are some things your government could do:

- You could send a share of your country's money to poorer countries. This is called 'aid'. Lots of rich countries do this and it can certainly help. It's not quite as easy as it sounds. It's tricky to make sure all the money will reach the people who need it. But there are lots of organisations, including the United Nations (see page 70), who can help. You could think hard about what the money you give should be spent on. It's obviously important that people get enough to eat. But poverty is very complicated and other things matter too: education, healthcare, protection from some diseases that are common in poor countries (like malaria) and making sure women and children are treated well.

- It is impossible for countries at war – whether that's war with other countries or war between different groups within a country[52] – to deal with poverty and all its complex causes (like poor health or bad government). When there's fighting in a country, every other problem gets ignored. It's worse than that: war makes all those problems far worse. This might sound incredibly obvious. But the truth is that some of the poorest parts of the world are also some of the least stable, meaning they are at war or close to being at war. What can you do about that? These are big issues and arguably none of your business. So there's definitely a limit to what you can do. But you could use your new fame to try to bring nations

---

52 This is called a 'civil war'.

together (perhaps at the UN) to look for ways to end conflicts. A small number of countries make most of the weapons required to fight a war. If yours is one of them you could think twice before selling weapons to another country if doing so will make a war last longer there.

- Poor countries are less powerful than rich ones and they have sometimes had no choice but to agree to unfair trade deals. You could make sure your country pays a fair amount for the things it buys from poorer countries. You could make it easy for producers from poorer countries to sell things to people in your country. And you could sell things made in your country to people in poorer countries at a fair price. Sometimes that might mean not selling things too cheaply. If a rich country produces more chicken than it needs, for example, it might be tempted to 'dump' its unwanted chicken on a poor country by selling it very cheaply there. That will be good news for people in that country (those who like chicken, at least) for a while, but eventually local chicken farmers will go out of business because they won't be able to compete.

These are three big things - climate, technology and poverty - which could shape the world during your time as a global leader.

Your advisors will, I'm sure, bring you regular reports about all of them and help you to understand what they might mean for your country, and your citizens.

These are not the only big things that will be happening around you. They may not even be the biggest (it's not always easy to tell).

You will need to keep an eye on arguments between nations and try to make sure you don't get dragged into one.

You should keep a look out for pandemics and think about how to handle them. We have all experienced one now and seen how much damage they can do. Some countries were not well enough prepared. There's no excuse next time!

When you're leader of a country there are, I'm sorry to say, an awful lot of things to worry about.

But there are lots of reasons to feel optimistic about the future too. A brilliant Swedish academic called Hans Rosling used statistics to show that the world is getting better.

That doesn't mean there aren't problems – or that the world is getting better equally for everyone (it isn't) – but lots of important things are definitely going in the right direction.

Hans used to say that the reason it doesn't always feel like the world's getting better is because we notice when things go wrong much more often than we notice things that go well.

Most of us are leading longer, happier and more comfortable lives than any previous generation in human history. Remember that next time your advisors bring you a long list of problems to think about.

Your job is to help your citizens adapt to changes (many of which may be changes for the better) and work with other countries on common problems. Perhaps you could remind your citizens from time to time that things might be better than they seem!

Here's a thought. Remember that manifesto you were working on, setting out what you believe and what you want to accomplish as leader? It would be a good idea to tell people how you plan to tackle these issues.

Your citizens are still waiting to hear from you. Maybe it's time you made a speech.

Since you took power you've been squirrelled away reading this book in your hot tub, being fed Haribo® by a duke, and all the while your citizens beyond the palace gates are milling around wondering what you've got planned for them. I think it's time you told them!

Come on, finish your manifesto, and let's set up some TV cameras so you can speak to the nation. Go back over the checklists at the end of each section so far, use the decisions you've made to shape your speech, and – when you're ready – turn to page 172 for some pro tips about how to get your message across. You only get one chance to make a first impression, so you need to get it right!

NEW COUNTRY 'TO DO' LIST:

Medals and honours

Most countries award medals or honours – sometimes called orders or decorations – to people they want to reward for doing something special.

These can be military awards for courage (like the famous Victoria Cross in the UK[53]) or civilian awards for exceptional service to a country (like the Bharat Ratna[54] in India). Some honours give the recipient a title like "Sir" or "Dame".

We all like it when our hard work or good behaviour is recognised. That's why teachers hand out stickers for good work. Medals and decorations are really just adult versions of

---

[53] The most recent Victoria Cross was awarded to Lance Corporal Joshua Leakey of the British Army's Parachute Regiment who ran through enemy gunfire in Afghanistan in 2013 while trying to help an injured comrade to safety.
[54] Recipients of the Bharat Ratna include Jawaharlal Nehru, India's first prime minister (in fact he awarded it to himself), and the cricketer Sachin Tendulkar.

stickers. Most grown-ups would be just as pleased to get a medal as their children would be to find a smiley face on their maths homework.

Do you want to reward soldiers who take great risks in battle? Do you want to reward scientists who discover new medicines which make us all safer? Do you want to reward people who do hard jobs like nursing which we all rely on? Or perhaps there should be an award for particularly brave or hard-working children?

Once you've decided, you'll need to give your awards names (some honours have quite odd names like the 'Order of the Bath'[55]) and design a fancy medal to go with it. How about the Order of the Golden Pangolin? No? Fair enough.

---

55 The Order of the Bath is a British honour which makes the recipient a 'knight' which means everyone calls them 'Sir'. The name comes from a medieval ceremony in which new knights were bathed in water. (Maybe they were a bit smelly under all that armour?)

TOP SECRET: MEMO FROM THE DESK OF THE LEADER

Let's log another load of decisions which will no doubt be discussed by historians years and years into the future (no pressure!). The following template might help jog your memory.

With the power vested in me as leader I have decided our nation's highest honour will be called:

[If you don't like the Order of the Golden Pangolin I can also suggest the Noble Garter of St Crumpet. But you may well have better ideas. (Let's hope you do.)]

and it will be awarded for:

[Explaining what your honours are for tells people what sort of behaviour you want to encourage. It really is exactly how teachers and stickers work.]

Now set out on your sheet of paper the top three things, in order of priority, you would like to try to help deal with:

Climate change
How technology is changing things
Global poverty

[There are so many other issues that will cross your desk. These three are just for starters. I could write a whole separate book on all the rest (note to editor: interested?). You could spend some time researching what they might be. We have mentioned the danger of arguments between countries and the threat of future pandemics.

Some of the other issues you could add to this list include: global health (poor countries have problems like a lack of vaccines, but rich countries have problems too, like obesity); demographics (this means how many people there are, where they live and how old they are – and it is creating massive change); and misinformation (social media has made it easier to spread lies around the world, and it's a problem if your population is unsure what's true and what isn't). Don't forget – not all the issues you need to deal with will be problems!]

PART SIX: NOTES FOR NON-LEADERS

This is a book for first-time leaders – specifically, children who have found themselves in charge of a country. I'm a very busy man and I don't really have time to write books for ordinary children.

In fact, if you're an ordinary child, I'd like to know why you're even reading this. Stop it! This book isn't for you. Go and do something ordinary children do like – I don't know – sticking LEGO® bricks up your nose[56].

---

56 LEGO® bricks are no better than crayons as far as the nose is concerned. Just don't stick anything up your nose, okay?

What? You're still here?

Well, I suppose there have been plenty of people in history who have changed the world for the better without ever being in charge, so you might not be totally useless. Inventors, musicians, poets, writers, business leaders, campaigners, artists, actors, scientists – lots of scientists – and, yes, even children.

Maybe you - even little old you - will find a way to make your mark, whether you end up in the presidential palace or not.

You can choose to be kind, forgiving, co-operative, persistent, resilient, honest and hard-working. You can try not to harm others, or the environment. When you see things that could be better – at home, at school, in your village or town – you could try to be heard. But how? Well, I'll tell you.

Noticing something that needs to be fixed is only the start. If you're going to do something about it, you need to act. That's much harder.

You will need:

Passion No-one will follow you if you're not passionate.

Courage Drawing attention to yourself can be uncomfortable and scary.

Persistence Change rarely happens quickly.

Strength You may have to stand up to people who discourage you.

Organisation You will have to make a plan and stick to it closely.

Listening skills You should listen to people who agree with you (in case they have useful experience or better ideas) and people who disagree with you (so you know why).

Teamwork You will be able to achieve more in a team than you could on your own.

A willingness to learn You will need to know a lot about the issues that matter to you.

Here's how you can be heard:

Petitions

A petition is a demand for change signed by lots of people. In the old days, you had to go around with paper and pen, door to door, trying to collect signatures. These days you can create an online petition using a website (like change.org or 38degrees.org.uk), which is far easier.

The hope is that with enough support – and some of these petitions have been signed by millions of people – your campaign will be noticed.

The UK Parliament has its own e-petition system. The European Parliament has the PETI online petition system. When a petition gets a certain number of signatures, the topic will be debated.

Don't forget that petitions have the power to create change anywhere, and sometimes it's not the government that needs to be persuaded to act.

If you want your school to commit to using less plastic, for example, you don't need to bother the prime minister. You just need to bother the head teacher.

Social media

A lot of parents worry about their children using social media apps like Twitter®, TikTok® and Instagram®. There is some evidence that social media and smartphones can make children anxious and stressed. But if they are used carefully, some of these apps can be helpful. They can allow you to reach a huge number of people.

Social media acts a bit like a giant petition; when lots of people use the same hashtag to support a particular cause, for example, the fact that people everywhere are talking about the same issue can make it difficult to ignore.

Make sure the adults in your life know what you're doing, though. Social media is a public space. Don't publish anything you might find embarrassing later on, and certainly don't share any private information (like where you live).

Writing letters

It's a bit old-fashioned, but writing letters can be a great way to get your point across. Proper letters, written well and sent through the post, are powerful. People find it hard to ignore letters (they are certainly harder to ignore than emails or social media messages).

Try your very best to be polite, respectful, clear, accurate (no spelling mistakes, please!) and remember to ask for a specific, positive action: what do you want the person you're writing to to actually do? It is also a good idea to say a little about yourself.

(But remember to keep your letter fairly short; you probably don't need to list all your swimming certificates and food intolerances.)

Protest

A protest – sometimes called a rally or a demonstration – is when people meet to yell, bang drums, hold up posters and call for the change they want to see.

Protestors usually meet somewhere significant, like outside a government building, and often march through the streets to draw attention to themselves.

It's possible to protest alone (that's how Greta Thunberg[57] started), but usually the aim of protest organisers is to get as many people as possible involved.

As long as protestors don't cause serious problems or danger to others, they are generally allowed to demonstrate as much as they like in free, democratic countries. In some countries, however, protest is illegal, and anyone who tries it is taking a serious risk.

Two types of protest have become very visible in the last few years: climate activists (like Extinction Rebellion) and anti-racist protestors (like the Black Lives Matter campaign). These two groups have done a very good job indeed of getting their important causes noticed.

You'll need to find an adult to go on a protest with you and you should encourage them to think about whether it's going to be safe. If it's a really large event (some protests are huge) it's a good idea to have a plan for what to do if you get lost or separated.

---

57 When Greta Thunberg was 15 she started skipping school to sit outside Sweden's parliament to protest about climate change. In 2019 she spoke to world leaders at the United Nations in New York. "For more than 30 years the science has been crystal clear," she said. "How dare you continue to look away and come here saying that you're doing enough."

Holding office

We've talked about how you could set about trying to influence people who have the power to help you with your campaign. But there is something else you could try, something so obvious you might forget to think about it. You could become the person with the power.

This book is – as you know – written for exactly that person: the young ruler of a new nation. If you're reading this section, that's not you. But remember there are other powerful positions you could aim for. Why not start with your own school council?

IT'S MANIFESTO TIME

You can't put this off any longer, boss. You've read the book (I mean … you have, haven't you?) and you've been tinkering with your manifesto since part one. You should also have five memos to help you by now. It's time for you to finalise your vision and present it to your people.

Now look, it's okay to feel nervous. Hardly anyone enjoys public speaking. But the people out there are on your side. They want you to do well. So be confident. Be clear. Be a leader. You know what you want to do. Now you need to explain it in clear, strong, simple and inspiring language.

What else can I say that might help? Well, don't talk too fast (you probably know that one), don't mumble (you probably know that one too) and look at the people you're talking to as much as you can. Don't just bury your face in your notes. And be yourself. I mean, look, not completely yourself… don't relax so much you burp or something. But talk in your own voice, smile your own smile, and try to enjoy it. After all, you wanted to be leader, remember?

That's why you took over the country in the first place. (I still don't know how you did that. I don't think there's any legitimate way for a child to take over a country. So it's probably still best I don't know.)

Okay. The camera's set up, the lights are on, I've loaded your words onto the teleprompter and we've brushed your hair. The TV networks are ready to carry you live to every corner of the nation on every channel. Ready? Three, two, one… and we're on air.

A LAST WORD

**Well, top dog, that's about it. I won't pretend
I've taught you everything. Running a country is
a complex business. Whatever plans you make,
you can be sure new problems and opportunities
will appear out of nowhere that neither you nor
I could possibly have predicted.**

That's why, in the end, what matters most isn't what you
know, but what you do. Your advisers can fill the gaps in your
knowledge. Only you can decide what you believe in and the
sort of leader you want to be. You need to make your own
mind up about how you want to run your country.

**Before you go off to enjoy being the most
important person around, there are three things
I think you should remember as you take charge:**

The first is that it's a good idea to **be kind**. That means
thinking about how your actions and decisions might
affect others and being quick to forgive those who are
unkind to you.

You won't please all the people all the time (remember?) and
some will not like you – that's politics, I'm afraid. But if you try
to treat people kindly, even those who do not agree with you,
you will be well on your way to becoming a great leader.

The second is simply that you will need to **work hard.** The most talented leader will achieve very little without working hard. History's very greatest leaders have always been both talented and hard-working. (As I've said, this formula works for everything.)

And then there's **courage.** Running a country (or taking on any responsibility) takes courage. Why? Because there is a chance you will fall flat on your face and look silly.

And that's scary, isn't it? People might laugh at you. But here's the thing: it doesn't matter if you fall flat on your face. And it really doesn't matter if people laugh at you.

Failure is not the problem (you can always try again). Not putting yourself forward for positions of responsibility because you fear failure, or being laughed at, is the problem. If you never try, you will never find out what you might have achieved.

Anyone you admire will have taken risks to get to where they are in life. And that certainly goes for leaders.

So be kind, work hard and have courage. I'll be watching with pride from the sidelines.

When you've got comfortable behind the huge mahogany desk in the Emperor's office, hung a few pictures on the wall and chosen your national animal (the pangolin, obviously), remember that the most important thing is to be yourself and to stand up for what you think is right.

You will find things out about yourself while you're in charge, things you didn't know before. That's what happens to leaders. They are tested by events and their true qualities are quickly revealed.

I'm pretty sure you're going to discover that you are easily kind, hard-working and brave enough to be the best leader we have ever had.

Acknowledgements

Writing this book felt like a big responsibility. What if, thirty years from now, we find ourselves living under the despotic rule of a wild-eyed tyrant who drew inspiration from these pages?

Well, if that happens, don't blame it all on me. Phoebe Jascourt got the project underway and Julie Ferris, Laura Horsley, Nigel Baines, Laura Hambleton and Kelly Llewellyn saw it safely – and expertly – through to publication.

It's been a pleasure to have Stephanie Thwaites and Isobel Gahan at Curtis Brown in my corner. And if you enjoyed this book it will have been in large part because Allan Sanders' illustrations are so brilliant. Thanks, Allan.

Emma: thank you for encouraging and supporting me in this (and so much else). Matthew and Patrick: this book is for you. You may or may not run a country one day. But I bet you change things for the better whatever you do and wherever you go. You've changed my world for the better already.